FENG SHUI
WITH WHAT YOU HAVE

Connie Spruill, FSII, and Sylvia Watson, FSII

Adams Media
Avon, Massachusetts

We dedicate this book to Nancilee Wydra and her contribution to the field of feng shui. Also to our husbands, Leonard Watson and Cliff Spruill, for their love and support.

Published by
Adams Media, an F+W Publications Company
57 Littlefield Street, Avon, MA 02322. U.S.A.
www.adamsmedia.com

ISBN: 1-59337-013-X

Printed in the United States of America.

J I H G F E D C B A

Library of Congress Cataloging-in-Publication Data
Watson, Sylvia.
Feng shui with what you have / Sylvia Watson and Connie Spruill.
p.   cm.
ISBN 1-59337-013-X
1. Feng shui. I. Spruill, Connie. II. Title.

BF1779.F4W37 2004
133.3'337—dc22
2003022380

This publication is designed to provide accurate and authoritative information with regard to the subject matter covered. It is sold with the understanding that the publisher is not engaged in rendering legal, accounting, or other professional advice. If legal advice or other expert assistance is required, the services of a competent professional person should be sought.
—From a *Declaration of Principles* jointly adopted by a Committee of the American Bar Association and a Committee of Publishers and Associations

Many of the designations used by manufacturers and sellers to distinguish their products are claimed as trademarks. Where those designations appear in this book and Adams Media was aware of a trademark claim, the designations have been printed in initial capital letters.

Cover photographs © Royalty-Free / Corbis
Interior illustrations by Catherine Sheridan

This book is available at quantity discounts for bulk purchases.
For information, call 1-800-872-5627.

Contents

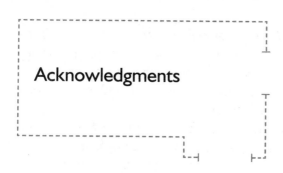

Acknowledgments

THIS BOOK IS A DREAM come true for both of us, as we are finally able to share our passion for feng shui and how it has changed so many lives. Being given the opportunity to write this book provided us with the platform we sought for years to demystify feng shui for the general public through sharing the philosophies of the Pyramid School of Feng Shui. We can now answer the plethora of questions posed to us by our clients and students and clarify misconceptions that many people hold regarding feng shui.

We give special thanks to our families, especially our husbands, Leonard Watson and Cliff Spruill. We want to acknowledge them for their patience while we worked into the wee hours of the night, broke away early from family celebrations to stay on schedule, and for their encouragement, their support, and opinions. To our grown children, we hope this book will help them understand once and for all what it is we do as they read the final copy and see some of their own situations shared within the book's covers.

Our gratitude also goes to a very special lady at Adams Media, Kate Epstein, for her enthusiasm, understanding, and discerning editing. She kept us focused and on track, forcing us to clarify every abstraction of our subject.

Catherine Sheridan, professional freelance artist extraordinaire, did all of the illustrations for the book. She is not only a very talented artist; she is also an extremely intelligent woman, as evidenced by her ability to understand the long-winded explanations that we provided in order to explain our ideas.

Of course, we couldn't forget our favorite critics, Monika Jones and Svetlana Pelova, who spent hours reading and rereading each chapter of this book. Their honest feedback forced us to reevaluate and rewrite many passages. Also thanks to Connie Faddis and Jennifer Ilitch, who were great sounding boards when writer's block occurred.

Feng shui students we have mentored, class participants, and especially our clients contributed immeasurably to this book unknowingly. Their poignant questions, inquisitiveness, and personal feng shui success stories set the stage for the outline of this book. Without them there would not be a book.

We save our biggest thanks for Nancilee Wydra, founder of the Pyramid School of Feng Shui and the Feng Shui Institute of America. We have been blessed by her eloquent approach to teaching this science and art. She has opened our eyes to a new way of experiencing life and we are better for it. We are grateful for her influence, guidance, and generosity, but most of all, for her friendship. Nancilee is a brilliant teacher, challenging mentor, thought-provoking writer, excellent presenter, and standup comic all rolled into one.

Most important, we want to recognize you, our readers, whom we believe will benefit from *Feng Shui with What You Have*. We hope this book becomes a trusted companion along your life's journey.

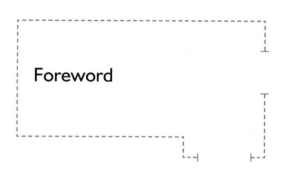

Foreword

THERE IS NOTHING SO GRATIFYING than to experience ideas growing to fullness. Before feng shui was little more than a speck of light in our culture's horizon, and no one in the West recognized the concept of how important the physical environment is to one's experience in life, I felt bereft that there was no one else with whom to share the work of shaping feng shui. I saw feng shui as the fourth and stabilizing leg on the foundation of the human experience. While Western consciousness now includes the awareness that mind/body/spirit are inexorably linked, it was my belief that, like a three-legged stool, mind/body/spirit was missing another leg. That leg was place—the messages of the physical environment that shape one's life experiences.

When the way to contemporize feng shui was only an embryonic seed, Sylvia and Connie joined this journey and I acquired two colleagues to share in the work of extricating the social and physical scientific explanations that would give feng shui a foothold in our rational Western world. I was truly blessed because these two women exemplify what was needed for feng shui to emerge as a contemporary social and physical science: an unerring sense of exploration, a colossal energy to learn, and the grace to lightly sew the threads of a developing field together. It is, therefore, with almost parental pleasure that I write this foreword for *Feng Shui with What You Have*. I know that the information disclosed comes to you with impeccable academic standards and is dispensed from loving hearts.

And so, dear readers, I leave you in good hands, knowing that this book will add immeasurably to the quality and context of your life.

Fondly,
Nancilee Wydra

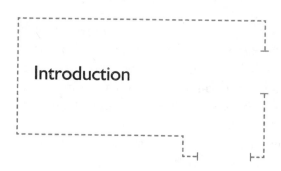

Introduction

What This Book Can Do for You

Feng Shui with What You Have draws primarily on the Pyramid School of Feng Shui, in which we are certified. While all schools of feng shui share certain core concepts, the Pyramid School of Feng Shui, founded by Nancilee Wydra, is the most contemporary school of feng shui. Drawing upon the classical schools and contemporary social and physical sciences, Pyramid feng shui incorporates Western culture and the effects of individual psychological issues. It also gives much attention to environmental issues such as the identification of toxins found in building materials and electromagnetic fields emitted from electronic devices, along with practical, safe alternatives.

In *Feng Shui with What You Have*, we have attempted to provide the tools to apply feng shui concepts without much fuss or expense. This book is going to teach you how to understand the language of the environment. We believe that feng shui is one of the most powerful systems available for effecting change in people's lives. Applying feng shui to your surroundings can help you land a promotion, find romance, support the self-esteem of a shy child, reduce stress, or increase prosperity. On a deeper level, it can remedy broken family communications or take a person from a lethargic, unmotivated psyche to an energetic, motivated ball of energy. Feng shui adjustments can even hasten a healing situation, making the difference between a short-term and a long-term recovery.

Applying feng shui means answering some key questions about your physical environment, such as:

- Who lives here? What does the environment reveal about the occupant?
- What negative culprits within the space are standing in the way of the occupant realizing his or her dreams, intentions, and goals?
- What remedies will allow the occupant to reverse her or his misfortune and to create a home that is fulfilling, inspiring, and healing?

Feng shui is about the interaction of a person and his or her environment; it's a two-way conversation. Sometimes your space speaks volumes about you, revealing present-day life challenges, while other times you take the podium by adjusting your space, which in turn affects how you feel and subsequently how you behave.

Feng Shui with What You Have takes the mystery out of why feng shui works, giving you insight, practical knowledge, and a purpose for adjusting your space a certain way. Having this knowledge will help you identify the positive reinforcement already existing within your spaces, while also helping you to identify symbols or messages that trigger negative emotions.

Section I will cover the ABCs of feng shui. With a working knowledge of the components of feng shui, you'll be able to use simple instructions with exercises to gain a mindset for the application of feng shui to your spaces. You will learn the strong role that your personal intentions play in the process.

Section II contains the "how to" chapters. What do you do first? Why do you do it first? How do you do it? Here you will train yourself to look at your physical environment with new "eyes" and a new attitude. You will ask yourself, "Why didn't I see this before?" or exclaim, "Oh my! The answer has been in front of me all the time." You will also discover how clutter impacts your life and holds you prisoner, preventing you from moving forward in life.

Section III contains room-specific situations supported by client examples. Discover how the principles of feng shui are also the foundation of good design. Easy-to-use tip lists will provide commonsense, no cost solutions for these specific rooms. You will begin to see the connection between poor room arrangements and the problems you are experiencing in your personal life, and you will come to realize why feng shui is truly a metaphor for living.

And in the final section, we leave you with client stories involving real-life situations that may hit a chord with you. Without a doubt, it will become obvious that when feng shui is used as an intervention tool, a person's quality of life is enhanced.

We hope you find this book interesting, educational, inspirational, and fun. Try to do the exercises as you read the book; this is as much an instruction manual as it is a hands-on, interactive experience. So, go and enjoy yourself. We hope it opens your eyes to new horizons and that you discover all that you can be. Blessings!

Section I
The ABCs of Feng Shui

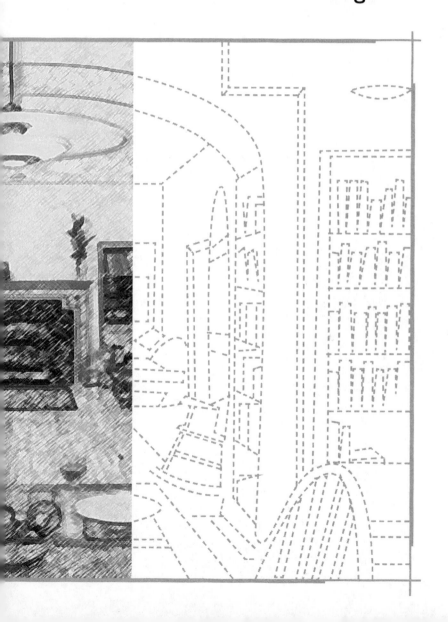

Chapter 1

The Power of Feng Shui

"... [F]eng shui adds layers of diverse disciplines with its goal of casting more and more light on the mysteries of how the physical world impacts the human experience."

—Nancilee Wydra

A CASUAL PERUSAL of the feng shui section at your local library or bookstore tells you that feng shui is a popular topic. You will find feng shui books for the office, for negotiating, for career enhancement, for the garden, for health, for children's spaces, for fashion, and even feng shui for *cats*! Some books take a deep philosophical slant while others take a lighthearted, fun approach.

If you read several books on the topic, you might also discover that there are numerous schools of feng shui, some of which contradict one another. One book might recommend that a crystal be hung while the next book never mentions such a cure. In fact, the more you read about feng shui, the more confused you might get. You are not alone. Feng shui's popularity has given way to a proliferation of various experts and approaches. Some books emphasize the nature aspect, while others focus on the design aspect of feng shui. These books often show dramatic before-and-after case studies, some involving expensive remedies. Because of this, there are many who believe that feng shui recommendations involve spending a lot of money.

But such is not the case in our feng shui practice. Although some clients choose to combine feng shui with a remodeling project, a large number of clients spend little or no money on the adjustments. While there will always be those who go overboard when applying feng shui cures, a savvy feng shui practitioner will know how to use what's on hand with amazing results. Feng shui can bring about effective and positive change, and you don't have to spend money to make it so.

Deciphering the Mystique of Feng Shui

It is clear to us that the general public has some misconceptions about feng shui. *Feng Shui with What You Have* is, in part, our effort to dispel some of the most potent myths and reclaim feng shui's logic, practicality, and power.

Myth: Feng shui involves elaborate or expensive changes.
Fact: Good feng shui can be achieved at little or no cost.

Myth: You have to hang crystals, bamboo flutes, or use Chinese decorations.
Fact: Your own accessories, art, and symbols will prove to be more potent, because they have personal significance and reflect your own taste.

Myth: Feng shui is obvious or garish.
Fact: Feng shui should never be out of sync with the taste and logic of a home's inhabitant. Feng shui remedies that are strikingly apparent and a dwelling full of trinkets are signs of a feng shui consultation gone wrong.

Myth: Feng shui makes your home look Asian.
Fact: Your home should reflect your taste, history, and heritage. If you are Asian, of Asian descent, or collect Asian art, then an Asian theme is most appropriate if you so choose; otherwise, an Asian theme is not any more feng shui than any other theme.

Myth: Feng shui is a religion, a fad, or based on magic.
Fact: Feng shui draws from Taoism, a Chinese philosophy. Philosophy is very different from religion. It is definitely not a fad; it's been around for more than 5,000 years. Although feng shui results seem magical, it draws upon the laws of nature and science.

Core Concepts of Feng Shui

Even though we are proponents of the Pyramid School of Feng Shui, we study, appreciate, and value all schools, including traditional feng shui from China and other Asian countries, along with various Western approaches. Although Western schools may not be a replication of classical feng shui, in reality, both the Western and Eastern approaches are valid because *each responds to the culture it serves.*

No matter which school one prefers, there are certain principles of feng shui that all schools agree upon. These philosophical underpinnings never change. The basics are:

- **Tao**—Living in "The Tao" (translated "The Way") means that we should never go against the laws of nature; instead, we should attempt to live in harmony with them. It also means recognizing our interconnections to the natural world, our families, friends, communities, the universe, and a higher power.

- **Yin/Yang**—is the theory of how complementary opposites compose a whole. Just as daylight (yang) and nighttime (yin) are opposites, both are needed to compose a twenty-four-hour day. In our environments, it is important to have aspects of both. Yin is described as dark, quiet, still, and small; yang is light, with sound, active, and big.
- **Chi**—is referred to as "the breath of life" or vitality. Some refer to chi as a feeling that permeates throughout a space; however, it is best defined as any influence that can be experienced through the five senses.
- **Five elements**—Feng shui defines the world using elements of nature: Fire, Earth, Metal, Water, and Wood. Each element has its own influence and identifying features.

In summary, the core concepts teach us about being integrated in the world we inhabit, living in sync with nature, and fully utilizing our senses. This is how feng shui brings about a new awareness of our surroundings and prepares us to create spaces that truly benefit and support us physically, spiritually, and emotionally. As a result, we learn to enjoy and interact with the beauty of what's along a pathway as we travel its course.

A Short History of Feng Shui

Feng Shui evolved in China through several millennia, developing in various schools and sects. There are more than a dozen traditional Asian schools or sects of feng shui, such as Flying Stars, Four Pillars, Eight Mansions, and East/West to name a few. The two main Asian schools, however, are the *Form School* and the *Compass School*. The Form School, a combination of meteorology, geography, and geology, studies the shape, size, and lay of land-forms. It came about as an effective way for people who lived in the mountainous regions of China to protect their dwellings from harsh winds and dangerous water. In fact, the words *feng shui* mean "wind water."

The Compass School developed as the Chinese moved away from the mountains to other areas of China that were less hazardous. The Compass School places importance on the compass directions, focusing on favorable and unfavorable directions in relation to a person's birth date. This school introduced the main components of feng shui as being the yin/yang theory, chi, and the five elements. As the Chinese people adapted in response to the changes in their religions, philosophies, agricultural systems, commerce, and politics, so did the practice of feng shui, as well it should have.

The Black Tortoise, the Green Dragon, the White Tiger, and the Red Phoenix

The Form School, the first school of feng shui, grew out of ancient Chinese mythology about celestial animals that protected people from hazardous weather and terrain. When the animals descended upon the earth, they took topological shapes. The ideal land site looks like an armchair, with the highest mountains (Black Tortoise) in the rear of the dwelling, the right side protected by smaller hills (Green Dragon), the left flanked by the smallest hills or trees (White Tiger), and the front allowing for a clear, unobstructed view (the Red Phoenix). Traditionally, the Black Tortoise is in the north, the Green Dragon is in the east, the White Tiger is in the west, and the Red Phoenix is in the south.

Although it is not always practical to situate one's dwelling facing south, the notion of protecting the back of a house or building, reducing exposure on the sides, and having a clear view of those approaching is as important today as it was 5,000 years ago.

Coming to America

Coming to America changed feng shui yet again in response to a completely different culture with a diverse set of customs, symbols, and traditions. Professor Lin Yun brought feng shui to America when he introduced the Black Hat sect of feng shui. Even though it is based on Tibetan Tantric Buddhism, Black Hat offered Americans the first version they could grasp. Black Hat deviated from the complicated astrological system practiced by traditional Chinese schools and offered easy to use remedies. It was also the first school to place a heavy emphasis on a client's intentions as they relate to the important "stations of life," as later described in this book. Sarah Rossbach, a Chinese language student who studied with Professor Lin Yun, translated many of his writings and wrote the first books on feng shui published in America. Without her elegant writing style and skillful interpretation, feng shui as we know it would not exist.

The *Pyramid School* of feng shui completed the job of bringing feng shui into the American twenty-first century by synthesizing wisdom and knowledge from all of the schools while filtering out cultural and geographical proclivities. This school places heavy emphasis on current social and physical sciences, returning feng shui to its original status of a science.

Even though feng shui has changed throughout the ages, traveling from the East to the West, the basic premise remains as relevant today as it was in ancient times: use nature as a guide to create environments where you feel balanced, inspired, and nurtured. This does not require large expenditures of money. Anyone can apply the principles without spending a dime and reap its rewards. Our ancestors used what they had on hand and depended upon nature to provide them with food, shelter, and other necessities of life. When it comes to recycling, modern people could learn much from their predecessors.

Why Feng Shui Works

Feng shui works because it has roots in science and follows the laws of nature. Some fields of study that support feng shui include geology, meteorology, cultural anthropology, molecular cell biology, neuroscience, cognitive science, physiology, and psychology, to name a few. Environmental studies also play an important role, as does alternative medicine and healing. Here are examples of certain disciplines and how they prompt feng shui:

Biology

As humans we are biologically wired to respond to our environment. Our five senses experience our physical surroundings, sending a plethora of messages to our molecules and cells. When these messages reach our cells, the body and mind react accordingly. This system often protects us from danger or injury, as in the fight-or-flight reaction. Often these reactions are involuntary and happen in an instant; you touch a hot pan and pull your hand away so you won't get burned. Other times we turn a particular direction as we hear the sound of a water fountain, or we twinge in disgust when we smell the odor of garbage upon entering someone's home. On a more intimate level, a child's laughter lightens the heart and soft fabric sends a message of comfort. According to Pyramid feng shui, the environmental conditions that surround us serve as the catalyst for biological human response, and the school's philosophy follows that principle with the idea that you can change behavior by changing the environment.

Medicine and Alternative Healing

Feng shui is considered a major branch of traditional Chinese medicine (TCM). TCM is grounded in the premise that our physical environment impacts our physical, emotional, and mental health. Some progressive American health facilities incorporate feng shui into their overall design scheme. Instead of a cold, sterile, medical atmosphere, patients are now comforted by nature themes, full-spectrum lighting that duplicates sunlight, enhancements that appeal to the senses, and positioning of furniture that allows for intimate and effective communication. Feng shui can promote healing in patients while they wait to see the doctor, and the positive effects will continue long after the patients return home.

Light, music, aroma, and color therapies, each directly connected to feng shui, also lend to healing environments. Each of these alternative practices allows for a more holistic approach to medicine.

Feng shui offers the best medicine available and at no cost. Open a window and allow fresh air to enter, pull back the drapes and soak in a nature scene, wake up early and listen to the birds as they sing their morning songs, and stand in the moonlight and observe the night sky. Depend less on purchased luxuries and instead relish the splendor of nature's bounty.

Bau Biologie

This discipline addresses pollutants, toxins, and electromagnetic fields inside a home or building. Feng shui labels unhealthy environmental conditions as being "extreme yin" (damp, mold infested, and stagnant) or "extreme yang" (hot, arid, and steamy). These are characteristics often found in structures with "sick-building syndrome." Such conditions give rise to an array of physical ailments, including respiratory and depressed immune system diseases; correcting them restores the health of a space and its inhabitants.

Bau biologie also promotes the use of natural fabrics such as cotton, wool, and linen, flooring made of wood, tile, cork, or bamboo, and the use of water-based paints. Using such items keeps our homes closer to how nature intended and free of toxins emitted from synthetic materials. Bau biologie is now part of many feng shui professional certification programs.

Psychology

Feng shui takes into consideration a person's belief system along with learned and emotional responses to both negative and positive aspects and experiences related to place. For example, a child who was made to play in a dark and damp basement on rainy days while at the baby sitter's may, as an adult, be repulsed at the idea of a recreation room in the basement. On the other hand, a person's pleasant memories of a seaside vacation may find artwork and decorative items depicting the ocean a necessary part of his or her décor.

As humans, the way we relate to symbols is woven into the fabric of our lives. Our response tells a story about what and to whom we are connected. Finding and supporting important connections is an integral part of feng shui; as practitioners, we strive to bring into a space symbols and objects that emotionally connect clients to a purpose and meaning in their lives. Mental health experts now support the theme of connectedness as research has shown that a sense of belonging can mean the difference between living a healthy, happy life or falling prey to mental illness and a shorter life span.

Numerous studies have found that people who receive emotional support from friends and family recover from illnesses more quickly than those who feel isolated from their support systems. Feng shui shows us how to embrace our interconnectedness, bringing into our environments all that is important in life.

Physics

Classical physics deals with energy or matter that is tangible, seen, and precisely defined, while modern physics, or quantum theory, deals with an intangible force or energy that is not seen or easily explained. Even though feng shui shares common ground with both, it is more in line with the newer, quantum physics. While the objects, colors, and symbols (tangible) within a home or apartment affect behavior, a person's intentions (intangible) are what significantly impact change. Simply put, once you, the observer, start to focus on your desires, the more likely you are to realize them. Direct attention given to intentions bolsters the power of feng shui recommendations. For example, feng shui adjustments made to bring about romance are made stronger if the person first identifies his or her intention. Our clients realize success the more they can connect their intention to the feng shui cures. The more they realize this, the more powerful the results.

A simple example of this theory is when we watch a fly constantly hitting against a closed window with the intention of reaching the outside, when its escape route could easily be accessed and its purpose in life fulfilled if it just repositioned itself to see the open door behind it (giving attention to intention). Thus, a person who is immediately confronted by a wall upon entering her home each time might feel as if she continually runs into barriers in life—that it is a constant struggle to get projects completed or to move forward. Repositioning the activity, such as entering the home from another door if possible, might be a feng shui recommendation that supports redirected intentions.

Primary Imaging

This new discipline uses the latest discoveries about the cellular structures and processes of the human visual system to develop scientifically based design techniques. These new, highly specialized techniques give architects, feng shui practitioners, and other design professionals a much clearer understanding than was previously possible of how to create pleasing spaces for different individuals.

Developed after more than a decade of research by interior designer and researcher Beverly Payeff, primary imaging provides a scientific basis for determining, among other things, a client's preferences in shapes, forms, color, and lighting within a space. As a design discipline it provides a modern, Western, scientifically based view of how the built environment relates to human perceptual and cognitive experiences. According to Beverly, advances in brain research have made it possible to correlate data about the operational processes of the eye-brain system with the processes of spatial design.

In layperson's terms, this means that we can easily change how we feel in a space, using what we have, by simply creating a different pattern of movement for our eyes and brain to process. An example would be rearranging pictures on a wall, giving our eyes a different rhythm to follow or creating a different shape in the design of the display so that we respond more favorably.

Environmental Sciences

A very important theory aligned with feng shui's focus on nature is the biophilia hypothesis. Introduced by Nobel Prize winner E. O. Wilson, it expresses a common theme shared by all environmental studies. Simply put, humans have a natural affinity to nature. We are genetically encoded; our connection to nature is engrained and enmeshed in our whole psyche and being. Our exposure, interaction, relationship, and harmony with the natural world are, therefore, not only part of our physical well-being, as research has shown, but also our mental health. Disciplines that support this premise are ecopsychology, environmental psychology, and ecological design.

Summary—Feng Shui's Alliance with Science

- Connect rather than react to your environment by fully engaging your senses (biology).
- Appreciate the true meaning of a healing environment (medicine and alternative healing methods).
- Value the use of natural fabrics and building materials (bau biologie).
- Understand the emotional impact of both negative and positive aspects of your living space (psychology).
- Believe in the powerful connection between your intentions and your environment in affecting change in your life (physics).
- Create spaces that incorporate individual design preferences with a feeling of security (primary imaging).
- Be environmentally conscious by connecting more with nature and using the earth's resources more wisely, *especially by using what you have* (environmental sciences).

Becoming aware of the advances in science as they relate to feng shui solidifies and strengthens the person-place connection. As you learn more about this two-way communication between you and your environment, you will be encouraged to look at your living space in a new way, heightening your awareness of your surroundings. You will discover that feng shui is so much more than moving furniture; it's about life and change. It's about tapping into the power of your surroundings in order to express who you are, to learn how to reach your potential, and to discover how to bring meaning to your life. It's about improving the quality of your life and enhancing your physical, emotional, and spiritual well-being.

Our Intimate Relationship with Nature

Living spaces that express our sacred relationship with the earth cultivate our personal growth because they are grounded in the universal principles of nature, which guide us and give order to life.

It is our contention that everyone has a sacred relationship with nature; the challenge lies in allowing your space to nurture that relationship. Chances are your life interferes with this kinship. Most people in Western countries spend about twenty-two hours indoors, many under artificial light, breathing recycled, stale air as we superinsulate our buildings, homes, and apartments. The sound of the television, furnace, air conditioner, and other household appliances drowns out the sounds of nature while artificial aromas replace the fragrance of grass and flowers.

At work, many people listen to the hum of computers and the buzz of fluorescent lights and find themselves in spaces with windows that don't open or, worse yet, have no windows, making scenes of nature a rare experience. On one hand, modern technology improves our lives; on the other hand, modern living seals us off from the outside world, creating an impoverished indoor environment.

For most of human existence, we have called the outdoors home. Nature is our ancestral birthplace. Feng shui posits that our exposure, interaction, and relationship with the natural world are crucial for health, happiness, and optimum living conditions. That is why one of the goals of feng shui is to imitate nature. The ancient Chinese civilization flourished due to the people's observation, study, and application of nature's laws and patterns. Their art, poetry, philosophy, and science idolized and revered the harmony found when humans aligned themselves with the ways of nature.

Feng shui can help you to harness the wonders of the natural world in order to cultivate and rekindle your sacred relationship with nature. Here are simple ways for you to do this:

1. Bring the outside into your living spaces by using indigenous nature items as decorations in your home or apartment. For example, if you live near the ocean, be creative with sand and shells. Idea: Fill one-third of a glass vase with sand, one-third with shells, and insert blades of tall grass, real or silk flowers, or other foliage you find attractive.

2. In areas of your home where there are no windows, display your favorite outdoor scenes from vacations or other events where you are enjoying nature's bounties. If you have a computer and scanner, enlarge a few photos and mount them on cardboard. Frame them if you like or create a collage with them. For a visual treat, place them where you least expect it, like inside a coat closet, in your laundry room, in the bathroom, or on the inside of one of your kitchen cupboard doors.

3. Throughout each day, Mother Nature creates a variety of different lighting scenarios. We should mimic these situations:
    - To duplicate full sunlight, use full-spectrum lighting in a windowless room or closet.

- Just imagine sunlight shining through tree limbs, drawing attention to a budding flower being visited by a butterfly, or natural light streaming through the leaves early in the morning, providing an ethereal view of nature. These effects can be duplicated indoors by setting up lighting behind plants or by diffusing light from lighting fixtures by placing lightweight fabric over a lampshade.
- To create the ambiance seen at dusk, light candles or hang miniature white blinking lights that mimic fireflies.
- To duplicate the golden warm glow of sunset, use a yellow incandescent light bulb in a table lamp.

4. For cleaner air, use plants that, according to NASA research, purify and remove indoor toxins. Palms, dracaena, English ivy, Boston fern, corn, and ficus plants are good choices.

5. Download your favorite nature scene as a screensaver.

6. Think clocks! Use chirping clocks that mimic birds, a cuckoo clock, or a Winchester clock with four different nature sounds every fifteen minutes.

7. At night, shut off the TV, radio, and stereo and open the windows. A breeze rustling through leaves, sounds of crickets, and the patter of rain are not only pleasant but actually serve to lower blood pressure.

8. Use a rock as a paperweight.

9. Use small fans to create illusive movements that mimic nature's breezes. Place them strategically where they will blow on a lightweight curtain or behind a plant to give the impression of a breeze.

10. Avoid monochromatic color themes. There are no nature settings that come in shades of only one color. Even the desert has a blue sky to contrast with the sand.

Even though we mention interior enhancements as an important part of connecting with nature, nothing takes the place of spending time outside. Make your outdoor experience a fun time: take your shoes off and walk in the grass; go rock collecting; play in the dirt; go on a nature hike; sit by a fountain; hug a tree; smell flowers; start your day by stepping outside for a few minutes, and at night, gaze at the sky and observe the path of the moon over the next thirty days.

Feng shui encourages and promotes your relationship with "the" nature by bringing physical reminders of the natural world into the places you inhabit, encouraging exposure to and experience with the outdoors, and by helping you benefit from the profound wisdom found in nature. Practice her ways: avoid extremes and stagnation. Instead, value balance and change. Be like Wood and try new things, be like Fire and reach out to others, be like Earth and nurture yourself, be like Metal and get focused, be like Water and go with the flow.

Mother Nature uses what she has; you can do the same!

Chapter 2

The Big Three:
Tao, Yin/Yang, and Chi

"By watching the many cycles of the physical universe . . . Chinese philosophers perceived a rhythm connecting humanity with nature and confirming that the laws of nature were also the laws of life."

—Angel Thompson

TAO, YIN/YANG, AND CHI ARE the core concepts connecting all schools of feng shui to their ancient Chinese roots. Understanding them sets the stage for using what you have to make feng shui work for you.

Connecting Us to Who We Are

Feng shui is based on an underlying respect and understanding that all things are connected and dependent upon one another. This philosophy is pulled from Taoism and supports feng shui's principle that all of life works effectively when all of nature's elements are balanced.

As humans, an invisible thread in the web of life connects us to not only the natural world but also to our families, our social networks, our professional teams, our cultures, our faiths, our beliefs, and our core principles, which enriches our lives as a result. In truth, it is this connecting thread in the web of life that makes us feel prosperous and abundant in all things. Just like fledgling beginnings and growth cycles in nature, we cannot fulfill our purpose in life without experiencing the full impact of this connection.

Try this Tao exercise: Go to a favorite spot in your home or outside. Take a good look around you. What do you see? What do you smell? What do you touch? What do you hear? Can you taste anything? With your eyes, take a snapshot of what you see. Now close your eyes. One by one, take away from your picture what you see, hear, smell, touch, and taste. Take away the light. How do you feel? Imagine living with this feeling most of your life. How would you correct this situation?

Sadly, many people in today's society live disconnected from many life-giving forces. Their dwellings lack any vitality. They close themselves up in their homes. Their windows stay covered. No portraits or keepsakes exist that might connect them with family or past memories. Absent are the aromas that bring back pleasant memories of their past.

Another challenge we face is our exposure to and reliance upon technology. On one hand, electronic equipment such as televisions, computers, and cell phones isolate, distract, and disrupt our interaction with others. This interferes with our innate need to belong and connect to people in our lives, a core foundation of civilization.

On the other hand, watching a sports event can be a fun time for family or friends, an e-mail can be a marriage saver when a spouse is serving in the military, and a cell phone can certainly be a blessing to a person stranded on the highway. It's important to balance the use of technology in a way that nurtures rather than hinders connection. The following chart shows how symbols can create connections.

SYMBOLS	CONNECTS YOU TO . . .	RESULTS IN . . .
Photographs	Loved ones	Feeling of warmth
Landscape poster	Nature	Healing; lightness
Pebbled walkway	Memories of childhood playtime	Going outside or taking a walk
Aroma of buttered popcorn	Memories of childhood visits to theater	Decision to re-create by going to a movie
Popular music from another era	Memories of school dances	Night out dancing
Awards, certificates, diplomas	Validation of accomplishments	Heightened self-esteem

Straddling the Scales—Yin/Yang

Yin/yang is the concept of interconnected opposites that complement and complete one another. We cannot experience light, for example, without knowing and experiencing darkness. Yin/yang explains the process of change, transition, and of cycles. The simplest example of this is that day (yang) turns into night (yin) over and over again. The chart on the right offers other examples of yin/yang seen in nature.

YIN	YANG
Sun setting	Sun rising
Dark clouds	Rain
Fall, winter	Spring, summer
Low tide	High tide

Following are examples of yin/yang experienced in our dwellings.

YIN	YANG
Dark colors	Bright colors
Curving paths	Straight paths
Areas where you rest	Areas where you are active
Items that are small	Items that are large
Dim lighting	Bright lighting

Yin/yang also applies to temperament and personality types. Most yin personality types (thinker, planner, mild-tempered) prefer to read, listen to music, and sit outside as ways to release stress, whereas those with yang personality types (active, people oriented, aggressive) find massages, walking, and soaking in water pleasant stress busters. Incorporating aspects of yin and yang into a dwelling is an integral component of any feng shui consultation. It brings a sense of health and balance to a space. Just imagine if all your rooms were dim and quiet or if all your rooms were bright and noisy. Need we say more?

WHEN YOU WANT YIN . . .	WHEN YOU WANT YANG . . .
Turn off the lights	Add light or wattage
Use a lamp for lighting	Use the ceiling light
Close drapes or blinds	Open drapes or blinds
Play soft music	Play loud, bouncy music
Light candles/stoke low fire	Create a roaring fire
Empty room of people and conversation	Fill room with people and conversation
Decorate using horizontal lines keeping the eye low	Decorate using vertical lines taking the eyes up
Neutralize fragrances	Add fragrances
Minimize accessories	Add accessories
Use undulating and curved shapes and forms	Include triangular and rectangular shapes and forms
Add nonreflective surfaces, nonglare glass	Add reflective surfaces, shiny tile, or mirrors to reflect light
Use flannel or other soft fabric	Use coarsely woven fabrics
Create slow meandering pathways	Create straight pathways

Our five senses are intrinsic to our experience of the yin and yang of a space. Some spaces in our homes lend themselves to high-energy activities (yang) while others lend more to relaxation and introspective activities (yin). The purpose and function of each space will determine if the space needs more yin influence or more yang influence. Keeping this balance in our surroundings contributes to the balance we need in our mental and emotional selves as well.

The chart on the facing page will help you understand how adjusting your environment impacts the yin and yang in a space.

Because you need the right mixture of yin and yang, it is important to know that the extreme form of either yin or yang creates its opposite. For example, being cold (yin) causes one to seek warmth (yang); if a room is too warm (yang) it causes drowsiness (yin); old stale food begins to rot (yin) and smell awful (yang); too much noise (yang) causes one to seek silence (yin); and too many stimulating colors (yang) causes mental exhaustion (yin).

The Winds of Chi

Chi—vitality or life force, is loosely translated by Westerners as energy. In our homes, chi is expressed or interpreted through the ambiance of a room or space. We experience chi through our five senses. We see and respond to color, shape, form, and pathways. We experience chi through aromas, both pleasant and not so pleasant, and through touch—smooth, textured, painful, hot or cold. We experience chi through taste—sweet, sour, dry, spoiled—and through sound—loud, soft, obnoxious, and so on. As we interact with our surroundings, the role that chi plays deeply influences our feelings. Many things such as the color of the wall, the pattern on a fabric, the density of the furniture, and the pathway through a room all influence the vitality of a space. And the level of that vitality dictates how we respond. Just as the speed limit and exit signs on the highway dictate our response on the road, the chi expressed by the elements in a room dictate how we respond in a space.

As our senses experience space, they affect our vitality, which is directly connected to our moods. Adjusting the amount of stimulation each of our senses experiences transforms those moods accordingly.

The following table will help you begin to experience the chi in your space.

MOVEMENT	SIGHT	SCENT/TASTE	SOUND	TOUCH
Pathways	Color	Aromatherapy	Nature	Smooth
People/pets	Line	Food smells/ tastes	People	Rough
Action pictures	Fabric	Fresh air	Pets	Soft
Breeze	Light	Stagnant air	Traffic	Plush
Rain falling	Shape	Chemical	White noise	Bumpy
Snow falling	Form	Mold	Voices	Sharp
Fabric at a window	Texture	Spicy	Water	Caress
Wallpaper pattern	Depth of field	Flowers	Machinery	Hot
Chimes/bells	Swinging mobile	Cologne	Music	Cold
Absence of movement	Absence of visual stimulation	Absence of taste/smell	Absence of sound	Absence of touch

Your Foundation

Understanding of the Tao, yin/yang, and chi are at the heart of feng shui. These three components serve as the foundation of all feng shui—without them, nothing else makes sense. Feng shui helps you make choices for your living space that promotes your well-being and happiness.

Chapter 3

The Five Elements

THE CONCEPT OF THE five elements—Wood, Fire, Earth, Metal, and Water—is an integral component of Chinese philosophy. These elements are the building blocks of the universe. Fire and Water are the catalyst elements as they instigate the shape and form of the other elements. Wood, Earth, and Metal are thought of as content elements as they represent the solid physical environment. Although each element can be defined by specific characteristics, it is crucial that they not be seen as fixed or separate from one another. These elements interact with one another; how they are combined explains why a space feels inviting or forbidding. Everything in existence, living or inanimate, can be categorized according to one of the five elements. As you learn about these powerful five, keep in mind that no one element is better than any other element; each should be appreciated for the assets and influence it imparts. For this reason, all five elements should be represented within a space.

Although we explain the elements in tangible terms such as color, shape, and materials, they have intangible effects on the mood, conversation, and even the behavior of occupants of a space.

The Elements—It's All about Change

Nature is always changing, following a certain order or cycle that explains all life processes. That life cycle is made up of a beginning, or emergence; a zenith, or most active phase; a waning, or slowing-down period; and an end, or period of dormancy. Each of these phases corresponds to one of the five elements. This process of change passes from beginning to end only to start over again.

To help you understand the process, let's take a look at the life cycle of a perennial flower, the day lily, as told through the five elements. Here's how the story goes:

The Wood stage: In spring the day lily pushes upward through the dirt and sprouts baby leaf stalks. At this point, the day lily is like a baby or toddler, full of energy, bending this way and that way, eager to grow. Learn from Wood's new beginnings: Be eager to pursue new endeavors, take a few risks, and be flexible.

The Fire stage: It is now summer and this beautiful flower is growing, blooming ever more colorful. The day lily is at this point like a teenager or young adult, full of life and growing. Learn from Fire's peak performance: Stay active, motivated, and inspired.

The Earth stage: The day lily reaches the midpoint, where for a short while, it's the best that it can be. As part of the life cycle, it is a time of transition and a time for pause. Just as

Wood is associated with spring and Fire is associated with summer, Earth's season is Indian summer, not too hot or too cold. Learn from Earth's stability and equilibrium: Stay grounded, centered, and balanced.

The Metal stage: Now the day lily wanes, relaxes, and starts to lose its color and shape. As fall approaches, cooler weather forces the flower's roots to contract and prepare for winter. Learn from Metal's preparation, concentration, and order: Be focused and let go of what is no longer useful.

The Water stage: With winter coming, the day lily has retreated into the ground where it lies dormant, in a deep slumber. Not to be mistaken for death, this stage of the life cycle is crucial as it allows the day lily the nutrients and rest that are needed before emerging again in the spring. Learn from Water's introspection, acceptance, and stillness: Honor what lies within, meditate, and remain still.

After winter passes, spring arrives again and the life cycle repeats itself not once but again and again. Learn to appreciate the process, trusting that change brings about what is needed to survive and thrive. Nature is a wise teacher. Just as the flower moves gently through the change process without resistance, we too need to embrace the inevitable flow of life. We are not meant to remain the same; if we do, we become stagnant, inflexible, and unhealthy.

Getting Down to the Facts

The five elements are important feng shui tools used to create desirable living and workspaces. For this reason, you need to know more about them. The more familiar you are with the elements, the more likely you can create a warm and friendly family room, a soothing and calm bedroom, or an inviting and alluring kitchen.

Each element can be described in terms of color, season, direction, shape, objects, movement patterns, influence exerted, and the list goes on. Following are characteristics that further define the five elements. We also include a way to use each element, or what we call a remedy, along with a word of caution for each. In this way, you grasp the meaning and essence behind the facts. It's like learning the definition of a new word. Although you can look it up in the dictionary, it's not until you hear it used in a sentence that you fully understand *how to use it properly*.

Wood

Color: Green

Shape: Rectangle or vertical lines

Objects: Any wood or green item; vegetation, plants, trees, flowers; cotton, linen, silk; artwork that depicts landscapes with trees, plants, or flowers; paper, cardboard; fabric with vertical stripes; fabric depicting flowers or vegetation; tall skyscrapers, wood fences, and decking; wood structures; rectangle-shaped tables

Season: Spring

Direction: East, where the day begins with the rising sun

Influence: Promotes change, beginnings, adventure, creativity, growth, healing and nourishment, achievement of goals, flexible thought and action

Life cycle stage: Infancy, or beginning

Quick Wood remedy: If you want to foster health and nutrition in your kitchen, create a table centerpiece by filling a large glass, bowl, or vase with any variety of greenery. Try something different by using asparagus stalks and fresh dill, along with any assortment of plant life, such as blades of tall grass, sprigs of fern, or wildflowers.

Caution: Don't bring too much Wood into an environment if you want to stay the course, encourage conservative thinking, and avoid risky endeavors.

Fire

Color: Any shade of red; reddish purple, magenta

Shape: Triangle, pointed shapes

Objects: Any item that generates heat; lamps, lighting, candles, and sunlight; people and animals; animal prints, real or faux fur, leather, suede, wool, and down-filled coverings; flame stitch and chevron patterns; any artwork depicting the aforementioned objects; pyramids, obelisks; houses of worship/buildings with steeples, spires

Season: Summer

Direction: South, associated with warmth of the sun

Influence: Action, motivation, and inspiration; promotes intellectual and spiritual pursuits; passion and understanding

Life cycle stage: Youth

Quick Fire remedy: If you need some romance and passion in the bedroom, burn some incense, light a candle, use leopard print sheets, add a small vase of red flowers, or place a red napkin under a lamp as an accent. Since Fire is the most yang of all the elements, a little goes a long way in a yin room such as the bedroom.

Caution: Refrain from using the Fire element if you want to encourage rest, steadfastness, or introspection.

Earth

Color: Yellow, peach, shades of brown, terra cotta, beige

Shape: Square

Objects: Clay, brick, ceramics, crystals, rocks, sand, and other products from the earth; earth landscapes; square-shaped tables and seating arrangements; basket weave or plaid fabric; brick buildings, square-topped, low structures

Season: Indian summer

Direction: Center

Influence: Sturdy, stable, grounded, centered; good at handling money, balanced, comforting; promotes trust and reliability

Life cycle stage: Midlife and transition

Quick Earth remedy: Want to create a warm and welcoming table setting for people meeting for the first time? Set an Earth-themed table by using ceramic plates with a beige tablecloth or beige place mats and napkins.

Caution: The Earth element should not be predominant if you want to evoke challenging or controversial conversation.

Metal

Color: White, ivory, gray, silver, or any metallic color

Shape: Round or circular

Objects: Any object made of metal; coins, pots, pans; gold, silver, or any metal-based jewelry; knives; metal trays and other serving utensils; round- or circular-shaped objects including tables; electrical equipment; fabric with circles or with a metallic sheen; concrete; buildings with domes, rounded arches

Season: Autumn

Direction: West, where the sun sets and daylight comes to an end

Influence: Letting go and endings; morality, ethics; precision, and systems oriented; control, concentration, and focus; appreciation of beauty and form

Life cycle stage: Old age; slowing down

Quick Metal remedy: If you are going on a job interview at a bank or accounting firm, bring out the gray suit with a tasteful piece of gold or silver jewelry (woman) or tie tack (man).

Caution: Do not use the Metal element if you want to invite creative thinking or if you want people to kick up their feet and relax.

Water

Color: Black or dark blue

Shape: Wavy and undulating

Objects: Glass, black, or dark blue objects; Water features such as fountains, bird baths; fabric with wavy patterns or swirls; curving and winding paths; artwork depicting the ocean and any water scene; buildings with undulating and curving roofs

Season: Winter

Direction: North, where the climate is cooler

Influence: *Still water* implies deep thought and introspection, wisdom, stillness; *moving water* implies communication and transmission, easygoing, yielding, able to circumvent obstacles

Life cycle stage: Ending; dormancy

Quick Water remedy: If your mind is racing and you need clarity, play music that has pleasant sounds of the ocean.

Caution: Too much of the Water element will inhibit lively, loud, and action-oriented behavior.

The Balancing Act

One of the goals in feng shui is to *balance the elements*. To bring about "balance" is paramount in feng shui. The elements can get out of hand when not combined correctly. If this is the case, a room may feel out of sync or you may not use the room as originally intended. If there is too much or too little of one element, then you need to correct the elemental mix. It all boils down to knowing how to combine them in just the right proportions—like a recipe that calls for a little of one ingredient but more of another.

So how do you balance the elements? To better understand how this is done, take a look at the following illustration; you will notice that the elements follow a certain order so that one element creates another element. For this reason, we call this the Creative Cycle.

The Creative Cycle:
Wood creates Fire,
Fire creates Earth,
Earth creates Metal,
Metal creates Water,
and Water creates Wood.

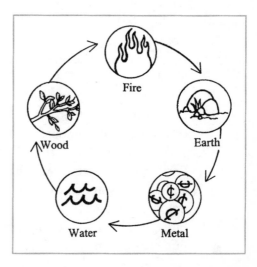

The Creative Cycle shows how the elements interact harmoniously. A room that has a predominant single element, a secondary element that stems from the first, and splashes of the other three elements will be harmonious. If you chose Earth as your predominant element and use Metal—the element created by Earth—as the next predominant element, with splashes of the other three, your room might look like this:

- Buttercream, yellow, and dark red plaid upholstered sofa and chair (Earth)
- Square-shaped coffee table (Earth)
- Dark tan carpet (Earth)
- Ivory-colored walls (Metal)
- Creamy beige drapes (Earth)
- Lamps with red-painted bases (Fire)
- Fireplace (Fire)
- Plants (Wood)
- Two rectangle-shaped wood end tables (Wood)
- Glass sculpture (Water)

This room will feel and look balanced because the elements are properly assembled. The reason for this is as follows:

1. The two predominant elements, being Earth and Metal, are beside each other in the Creative Cycle and therefore considered harmonious.
2. There is more Earth than Metal. In the Creative Cycle, Earth creates Metal much like a mother gives birth to a child. Just as in life, the mother should control the child, not vice versa.
3. Fire enhancements strengthen the Earth element because Fire creates Earth.

4. Wood and Water are used in smaller amounts; however, they are important because all five elements need to be present. If Wood and Water weren't in the room, it would seem mundane.

The following table provides guidelines to help you augment an element.

If You Need More . . .

Wood	Add Wood or Water enhancements (Water creates Wood)
Fire	Add Fire or Wood enhancements (Wood creates Fire)
Earth	Add Earth or Fire enhancements (Fire creates Earth)
Metal	Add Metal or Earth enhancements (Earth creates Metal)
Water	Add Water or Metal enhancements (Metal creates Water)

Mitigating an element depends on two other sequences: the Reduction and the Destruction Cycles. If you remember, we compared the Creative Cycle to a mother creating a child. The Reduction Cycle acts like a child who exhausts or weakens the mother. The Destruction Cycle acts like a father disciplining the child. The two cycles are as follows:

REDUCTION CYCLE
- Fire reduces Wood (Fire burns Wood)
- Wood reduces Water (Wood drinks from Water)
- Water reduces Metal (Water erodes Metal)
- Metal reduces Earth (Metal compresses Earth)
- Earth reduces Fire (Earth smothers Fire)

DESTRUCTION CYCLE
- Wood destroys Earth (Wood absorbs nutrients from Earth)
- Earth destroys Water (Earth dams Water)

- Water destroys Fire (Water puts out Fire)
- Fire destroys Metal (Fire melts Metal)
- Metal destroys Wood (Metal chops Wood)

With knowledge gained from the Reduction and Destruction Cycles, you are now able to reduce, or mitigate, an overabundance of any one element. If, for example, a room has white walls, white ceilings, and a light gray sofa and chair set, we would determine that the room has too much Metal. You can either introduce some Fire (from Destruction Cycle) or bring in some Water (from Reduction Cycle). If you use Fire features, you might place a red throw on the gray couch and add a red, triangle-patterned area rug. With these additions, you will create a look that is dynamic, eye catching, and tension filled. You might feel uneasy if you had to be in this room for a long period of time; however, it would make for a striking reception area of an interior design studio. Using the Destruction Cycle to lessen the effect of an element is a bolder remedy.

If you use Water features, you might use a black throw on the gray couch and add a black and gray wavy-patterned area rug with a few small swirls of beige and red. With these additions, you will create a look that is more harmonious, attractive, and inviting. Using the Reduction Cycle to lessen the effect of an element is a gentler remedy. Of course, all five elements need to be present in either scenario; otherwise both rooms would look stark and incomplete.

Room Review

Here's a great exercise we use in our classes to help students identify the elements within a room. Scan through magazines that you have on hand for pictures of rooms. We find magazines devoted to specific rooms, such as kitchens and baths, the easiest with which to work. If you don't have any, go to your local library or ask your friendly dentist for his or her leftover magazines. See if you can determine the predominant element. After that, check to see if you can spot the other elemental features in the room. Refer back to the section "Getting Down to the Facts" (page 27) in this chapter for the characteristics of each of the elements. Here are a few tips:

- Check the large areas first (e.g., walls, ceiling, and flooring). If the walls and the carpet are beige, then that room has a large amount of Earth. If the floor is wood and the furniture and the walls are green, the Wood element reigns supreme.
- If you need a system to follow, first look for Wood element features, then Fire, then Earth; afterward, spot the Metal features and, finally, Water.

So, now take a look at your room. If, for example, it is apparent that you have way too much Wood, a good rule of thumb is to first remove some Wood features or try to reduce the Wood by bringing in some Fire enhancements. Next, bring in some Earth and then a small amount of Metal. The last element to bring in is Water. Use Water sparingly in this situation, because Water creates Wood and would only aggravate the overabundance of Wood. (Refer to the Creative Cycle illustration, page 33).

Just as in learning any new skill, the more you practice, the better you get. Also remember that you may have to review this chapter a few times in order to become familiar with the information.

Chapter 4

Goals and Intentions—
Taking Charge of Your Life

"You cannot solve the problem with the same mind that created it."

—Albert Einstein

CLEAR INTENTIONS MAKE for powerful magic when connected to symbols in your life. Add to that the support you get from your surroundings and you have a winning formula for success.

Your dreams and intentions become the fuel that activates change in your life and serves as the catalyst for feng shui recommendations. Sparks fly when you connect your intentions with your living space.

Some think that feng shui is magic. It is not. So what makes feng shui work like magic? Maybe you've read about some feng shui miracles: a desk is moved and a promotion comes about; clutter is cleared and a new love interest enters the picture. What may not be understood is that before the result was realized, the intention was identified and the mindset changed.

Feng shui literally translated means "wind water." The wind is an unseen force of nature directing changes in the landscape. Your intentions are like the wind, an unseen force directing your life.

They symbolize your inner world of thoughts, dreams, goals, and desires, the part of you that is not seen. The second word in the translation is "water." Water is the visible force of nature that represents your outer surroundings such as your home and workplace. Like the ever-changing forces of wind and water in nature, your inner and outer worlds are also constantly interacting with one another. Conflicting interactions between wind (your intentions) and water (your surroundings) yield turbulent and sometimes destructive situations. The most beneficial results come about when the two are aligned, working in sync.

Even though we use the terms *intentions* and *goals* throughout this chapter, they are not the same. Intentions are broad in scope and refer to what you want to achieve. "I want to improve my health" or "I want to be financially independent" are examples of intentions.

Goals are specific, detailed objectives attached to a time frame. "I want to lose fifteen pounds in the next four months" or "I want to pay off two credit cards within the next twelve months" are examples of goals.

It is best to give thought to both intentions and goals. Intentions take you in the right direction while goals help you fine-tune your intentions. If you start with intentions, goal setting will be easier.

If We Could Grant You Three Wishes, What Would They Be?

You might be thinking, *How do I clarify my intentions? I'm uncomfortable making wishes;* or *I feel silly.* Think of envisioning your intentions as a brainstorming session about your life. Brainstorming is done in corporate boardrooms to generate goals, strategies, plans, and systems. It's a time to be creative and innovative. The feat of accomplishing goals and realizing intentions is no different in your personal life.

You may experience difficulty or frustration as you work to clarify intentions or make wishes. You might feel guilty wishing for something for yourself or find it difficult to prioritize the time needed for such an introspective, soul-searching activity. It's easy to get caught up in fast-paced living, taking care of everything and everyone while giving little attention to yourself. Somewhere along the line, you either don't give attention to planning your path in life or you let your hopes and dreams fall by the wayside, deciding not to pursue them.

Even with intentions and goals in hand, making them happen can also pose a problem. Taking action demands change and change can be overwhelming; fears may surface. After all, you will have to deal with unhealthy behavior, lifestyle, and habits; some of this change may even anger those in your immediate circle. Whatever the situation, you never move forward if you don't take action.

Feng shui offers a positive approach when focusing on your personal desires, taking away the fear of making changes and alleviating the uneasiness you might experience. For example, when a career change is your intention, the outward feng shui symbols applied to the environment can support the internal changes you encounter.

Your favorite yellow citrine paperweight that you've had since college can help in your new career endeavor. The color of yellow is good for focus and a paperweight is firm and grounding. Placed on your desk, this symbol may be the impetus needed to stay the course and finish your resume. What a simple yet powerful approach in reaching your intended goal. When aided by your environment, your desire for a new career becomes doable and less daunting. Reaching your goal becomes a journey with many adventures along the way. Make it worthwhile and give yourself permission to listen and act upon your heart's desires.

Give some thought to your dreams—they will help you clarify your intentions. Now it is time for you to begin your feng shui journey by choosing three wishes. If making wishes is not the approach you want to use, then set three goals. Some of our clients have a clear understanding of what it is they want in their lives while others are vague and lack direction. Whether you know what your three wishes are or find it difficult to come up with one, it is worth your time to try one or all of the following suggestions:

1. *Choose a notebook to record your wishes.* We recommend a small spiral-bound notebook so you can easily take it with you wherever you go. Make a list of wishes and desires that pop into your mind throughout your day. Don't limit yourself to writing down only three goals or wishes; go for the gold and record as many as you want.

2. *Set a timer for fifteen minutes and write a list of everything that you might wish for, no matter how fantastic.* Don't stop your pen until the timer goes off. Repeat this at least twice at different times of the day and week. Don't prejudge an entry because you don't think it is possible to achieve or currently lack the resources to make it happen. Prejudging sets up mental barriers that stand in the way of attaining your goals.

3. *Physical exercise can free your mind.* Sit down to make a list immediately after a brisk walk or other kind of workout. If you go to the gym, put your notebook in your gym bag and write your list in the locker room. If possible, don't wait until after you take a shower; for many people that puts them back into a workday frame of mind.

4. *Put some paper and a pen on your nightstand and write your list right before you go to sleep.* This may help you to be receptive to messages received as you dream. It will also keep you focused for the next day's activities as you gain insight about your intentions and goals.

5. *Just before you fall asleep you enter a highly suggestible state called a beta state.* Tell yourself you're going to dream about the perfect life for yourself. The next morning, write down anything you can remember about your dream. Even if you don't often remember your dreams, you may remember more than you expect if you're planning to write them down. Do this for a week and then read over what you've written. Try to identify aspects of the happy dreams and, conversely, aspects of the sad or frightening dreams. Become aware of the recurring themes and similarities. By doing this you will discover clues to your passions and aspirations along with your fears and come to realize parts of your life that otherwise would go unnoticed. This exercise has been known to help people unlock the parts of their mind that create barriers to achieving success.

Now that you have accumulated several lists, look for the common themes within them. Do they center on relationships, health or lifestyle issues, career or money problems, or some other issue? You may come up with five, ten, or maybe more common themes. Start prioritizing your themes by crossing out the least important ones until you end up with the three that are most important to you. If you have difficulty identifying those three, read your lists slowly, visualizing yourself achieving each goal, and see which visualizations make you the happiest. Perhaps you felt not only happy but also afraid when you visualized a particular goal. Stare these fears down, and realize that you are deserving of your goals.

Supporting Your Three Wishes

Once you have identified your three wishes, you must believe that they are achievable. Making a firm commitment to your intentions is essential before incorporating feng shui cures into your environment.

One of the most effective ways to dedicate yourself to your intentions is through the use of affirmations. An affirmation is a positive message you give yourself; it is another way to right the wrong scripts you've allowed yourself to embrace. Here are a few specifics as to how you write an affirmation:

- Always write an affirmation in the present tense, as if it is already true. Instead of stating "I will . . ." or "I'm going to . . . ," say "I am . . ." or "I (followed by a present tense verb) . . ." Here's an example of how you should write your affirmation: "I attract healthy relationships into my life."
- Always use "I" or "my" in your statement. In this way, you take ownership of your intention by connecting yourself to your affirmation.
- Always use positive language, affirming what you want to happen. Negative language leads to negative thinking. Instead of saying "I am not going to fear rejection," say "I grow from all of my experiences."

  Here are a few more examples of how an affirmation should be stated:

"I am worthy of abundance in all areas of my life."

"I feel confident when speaking to others."

"I attract mentors that provide me with guidance."

"All the cells in my body are healthy."

Now that you have a better understanding of how to create your positive reinforcements, compose an affirmation to support each of your three wishes.

Uncovering Obstacles

It's important to keep a positive frame of mind. Likewise, it's also necessary to rid yourself of the fears and obstacles associated with your intentions. Otherwise, you harbor resentments and anger that will nag at you, causing you to doubt your ability to bring positive change into your life. Here's a quick yet effective exercise that will help you purge yourself of your personal blockages:

• Write one of your wishes at the top of a page and, using your timer again, spend fifteen minutes writing about all negatives associated with attaining your goal. This might include identifying habits and behavioral patterns that you will have to let go of in order to achieve your goals. For example, if you want to go back to school but think you can't handle the test taking, you need to realize that this is a common first response. Recognize it as an excuse that lacks merit. If you still believe your rationalizations, then discuss them with a professional. Deal with each of your fears one by one. Often you'll find that your fears are learned perceptions that can be changed. Fears impair your potential for success and happiness; it is in facing your demons that you find courage to pursue your dreams.

• On another sheet of paper, at the top of the page, write down one of your three wishes (do this for each of the three wishes). For the purpose of this exercise, let's use returning to school as your wish. Under that, write the word *Benefits* and list how you would benefit if you obtained your degree or completed a training program. The list might contain: better paying job; work in a field I love; be a positive role model to my child; and feel personally accomplished.

• The last step is to cross out each benefit and contemplate the cost of not realizing your goal or wish.

How Feng Shui Becomes Your Fairy Godmother

Feng shui strives to redirect thought patterns and behavior by incorporating the appropriate symbols or enhancements into your environment that remind you of your desired changes. Your subconscious mind uses the five senses to process messages continually from your surroundings. That is why it is important to scrutinize your living space in order to find and eliminate what negatively impacts you and replace them with symbols that create a positive influence. The following story explains this message.

✳ Client Story: Granting Loren's Wish

Loren, a successful marketing consultant, was bored with the industry she'd worked in for twenty years, and the companies with whom she did business were downsizing. The industry was changing and so was the market. She now had to contend with more aggressive competitors who offered lower consultation fees. To make matters worse, she had not planned properly for retirement and she would soon be fifty. Although she admitted to losing interest in her field, staying self-employed was important to Loren. The problem was that she had no idea what she wanted to do. Her mind kept hopping from one business idea to another but never stayed focused on any particular one.

Before we could help Loren we first had to get her focused so she could identify her intentions; then we could make the necessary feng shui adjustments. Ironically, Loren had spent the last twenty years providing guidance and advice to business professionals, yet she didn't have a clue as to what to do for herself.

Since Loren was drawing a blank about her future goals, we suggested that she write down words or phrases that described how she would design her ideal future. Her list consisted of:

- New career that had no cap on earnings
- Flexibility with her time
- Freedom to choose with whom she worked
- Contributing to and helping others
- Fun, travel, and relaxation
- Comfortable retirement

We suggested that she think about some professions that matched her desired career features. She quickly answered, "Marrying a millionaire would solve my problems!" to which we responded, "Why not become a millionaire?" Loren laughed and shook her head as if to say, "Yeah, sure—me become a millionaire." Bingo! Here was a major stumbling block for Loren; she couldn't envision herself as a wealthy person.

After pointing this out to her, Loren gave some serious thought to why she never saw herself as being wealthy. To summarize the process, Loren redirected her thoughts and attitudes and dealt with her fears and misguided perceptions. She then discovered her intention: to have an enjoyable career helping others while earning substantial income. It wasn't important for Loren to be more detailed; the specifics of the career would surface in due time. Once she felt comfortable with her intention, we helped her develop a supporting affirmation. She wrote, "I am worthy of happiness and wealth and can have both while serving others." Wow! What a turnaround. Loren was now ready for feng shui recommendations.

Here is a list of the problems we found, followed by the recommendations:

Problem: An uninviting and nondescript entry: *Loren was unmotivated with no clear direction for her life. She needed to create a new door of opportunity.*

Recommendation: Use healthy plants to make the entry feel and look fresh and inviting. Place an unused small fountain, which Loren had tucked away in a closet, near the plants; the flow of water perpetuates the flow of new ideas. Position a small area rug at the entry to imply a strong foundation from which to launch her new career direction.

Problem: Living room in disarray with only half the room painted; various areas filled with clutter: *Loren had unfinished business and her vision for the future was blocked.*

Recommendation: Clean and remove the clutter from the living room. It's important to remove whatever creates an obstacle. Physical clutter leads to mind clutter. We suggested Loren paint the living room an earth tone color such as taupe or a variation of tan. The Earth element in an environment can be very grounding and provide a sense of security, which Loren needed during her career transition.

Problem: Two pictures, each displaying an entry and pathway to a garden, were on the floor, leaning against the wall upside down: *Loren, usually a very focused, upbeat person, was sidetracked with no sense of direction.*

Recommendation: Hang the two garden pictures in her entry where she would see them upon entering her home. Seeing pathways would prompt her along a new career path.

Remember the pictures were once on the floor? Such positioning denotes a status of low importance; hanging them elevates their significance.

Problem: Numerous plants scattered throughout the home, many of which were unhealthy and dying: *Loren was emotionally and mentally scattered and needed nurturing.*

Recommendation: Position plants so they receive proper sunlight. Fertilize, trim, or replant them if needed. Remind her that taking care of plants is like taking care of herself. Revitalized plants will help revitalize her dwelling as well as her mindset. Any dead plants were given back to the earth by mulching them into the outside flowerbeds. Last but not least, group some plants together to introduce the notion of her need to network with others in her new pursuit.

Problem: Too many Fire element items that included a deep red couch, lots of candles, and large, south-facing windows; too much Fire can result in a lot of activity without results: *Loren felt she was hopping from one forest fire to another leaving nothing but ashes where ideas once took seed.*

Recommendation: Take the beige chenille throw from her bed and place it over one side of the red couch to tone down the Fire element. Shield the south windows during the heat of the day by turning the miniblinds up, thereby still giving light but reducing the hot, dry effect from before. Also, move a silk tree in front of the window with the most glare, to further diffuse the afternoon sun. Last, move a small water fountain from a kitchen counter to an end table in the room. Nothing cools a hot Fire like some Water.

As a final recommendation, we asked Loren to frame her affirmation, "I am worthy of happiness and wealth and can have both while serving others," in a brass frame and place it on the credenza under the pictures of the garden paths in her entry.

Although she was not sure what would result, Loren applied all the cures. Within days, Loren reported feeling more focused, less stressed, and more comfortable in her new surroundings. The change in her environment helped Loren focus on a plan of action, which included researching various fields that met her criteria of an ideal career. Within a week she decided on financial planning, a field where she not only could earn a good living but also learn how to attain her own financial freedom. "This feels so right," Loren shared.

A year has passed and Loren is enjoying her designation of financial advisor and a high five-figure income. She is not only creating wealth for herself but also for others. We are looking forward to hearing about her millionaire status in the near future.

Loren proved that a person's mental energy can be changed from negative to positive when clear intentions are incorporated with feng shui recommendations. Know that your intentions or wishes can become reality when you make up your mind to pursue them and adjust your surroundings to support them.

Summary—Questions to Ask Yourself When Seeking Change

Do you have the courage to pursue new paths in your life that will inevitably change your future?

Are you willing to invest concentrated effort in this pursuit?

How willing are you to learn from the experience and wisdom of others?

Are you able to change course if you venture down the wrong path?

What in your environment redirects your focus to less important priorities and could be removed?

What meaningful symbols in your life can you incorporate in your surroundings to support your new endeavors?

Chapter 5

The Bagua—What's Life Got to Do with It?

"An understanding of how it [bagua] works will give you clues as to how you can create new possibilities in your life."

—Gina Lazenby

FENG SHUI DIVIDES all that is important in life into eight categories or "stations of life." They are:

- Self/career
- Wisdom/knowledge
- Community/elders
- Empowerment/wealth

- Future/fame
- Relationships/marriage
- Legacy/children
- Compassion/helpful people

A visual tool known as the *bagua* will help you to focus attention on each of the eight essential life objectives with the help of the physical environment to reach the final reward of mental, physical, emotional, and spiritual health.

The bagua is a template that can be placed over a house or room. We find a grid that looks like a tic-tac-toe board the simplest to use. By placing the bagua grid over your home or a single room, you can assign a life station to a specific area. The grid's middle area, the ninth zone, is used to represent health and is the only area that touches all of the eight aspirations. Think of it as the connector station that reinforces the theme of interdependency.

South

The bagua

Empowerment	Future	Relationships
Wealth	Fame	Marriage
Community		Legacy
Elders	Health	Children
Wisdom	Self	Compassion
Knowledge	Career	Helpful People

◄──────── Front of Bagua ────────►
or North

The top name of each sector is more congruent with contemporary, Western culture according to the Pyramid School. The bottom name is more in line with the Asian culture and traditional feng shui. The biggest difference in the names is that the contemporary language allows for a broader interpretation of the person as a whole. For example, in the case of empowerment/wealth, empowerment encompasses the idea that abundance can represent more than just monetary wealth.

Traditional feng shui places the bagua grid so that each sector is aligned to a certain direction of the compass; Western schools align the front part of the bagua along the wall containing the entry door.

To use the Western method, place the front part of the bagua (contains the wisdom/knowledge, self/career, and compassion/helpful people sectors) along the wall containing the main entry of the house, apartment, or room.

What is the entry door? Some assume that it is the front door; however, if you don't ever use the front door when you enter your dwelling, then the front door is not the main entry door. Choose instead the entry door you most often use to align the bagua.

To use the traditional method, position the self/career sector due north; this automatically places the future/fame area due south. The entry door will be aligned to any one of the eight directions.

HOW THE BAGUA FALLS UNDER EACH METHOD

BAGUA STATION	LOCATION IN ROOM (WESTERN)	LOCATION IN ROOM (TRADITIONAL)
Self/career	Bottom center	North
Wisdom/knowledge	Bottom left corner	Northeast
Community/elders	Middle area of left side	East
Empowerment/wealth	Left upper corner	Southeast
Future/fame	Upper middle area	South
Relationships/marriage	Right upper corner	Southwest
Legacy/children	Middle area of right side	West side
Compassion/helpful people	Lower right corner	Northwest
Health	Center	Center

Most of our clients choose to use the Western method. Directions have little meaning to the Westerner as it relates to life choices or positioning of a house. In fact, many in the West are directionally challenged. If it weren't for the fact that the highways and streets are labeled, we would be lost. We also find that builders and buyers in Western countries give virtually no priority to directions, so the traditional method of placing the bagua may seem awkward. If, however, your culture or belief system relies heavily on the use of directions, then use the traditional method. Again, feng shui should respond to you, the individual.

Using the Bagua to Identify Missing Areas in Your Home

Sketch the layout of your home or apartment on a piece of paper, including outdoor elements such as porches and patios. (If you live in an apartment, do not draw the layout of the building, only your apartment.) It is helpful to include doors and windows.

If your home is a square or a rectangle, all of the stations will be represented; if your house or apartment is an odd shape, then one or more of the stations will be missing from your house, as in the case of an L-shaped home. It is possible to complete the missing station using a physical feature that completes the missing section; this is done in order to alleviate problems with that specific aspiration. The following illustration may indicate an isolated person who finds it difficult either to ask for help or to extend a helping hand to others. The occupant could complete the bagua by planting a tree or placing a potted plant, or flat stone or rock at the intersection point in the missing area.

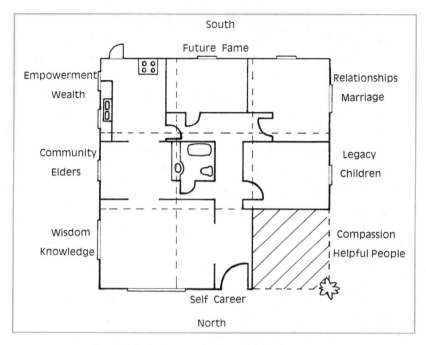

A potted plant is used to complete the missing
compassion/helpful people station.

If you live in an apartment that has a missing bagua station and feel that you don't have the option of making the necessary corrections to the exterior of the unit, think again; there are ways to mitigate a missing station even if you are not the property owner. A traditional feng shui approach would be to visualize an invisible line that outlines the missing station. Choose a small stone or other item that can easily be placed in the ground at the intersecting points of your visualized outline to complete the missing sector. Tie your intention of creating the missing sector to the action. You could also draw the outline of your apartment on a piece of paper and conclude by drawing the missing station with dashed lines. Next, write a positive affirmation related to the missing station. For example, if the relationship sector is missing, then you might write, "I attract healthy and loving relationships." Fold this paper and place in a small container, under a bowl, or behind a picture that is in the station next to the missing area.

Many people are confused as to whether they should place the bagua over their entire house or apartment or whether to place it over each room. You can do both. The main reason that you super-impose the bagua over your house or apartment is to see what sta-tion(s) is (are) missing and then to correct the situation. In this way, you address a negative aspect of your dwelling; it is a protec-tive response. You use the bagua over each room in order to incor-porate meaningful symbols, decorative features, and colors that have a direct correlation to each specific station of life. Here you take a proactive, positive approach by incorporating significant items into your environment that are directly connected to each important aspect of your life. For this reason, Pyramid feng shui places more importance on implementing the bagua to a room.

Using the Bagua in Every Room

Maximum benefit is achieved when you use the bagua over each indi-vidual room, but first you must decide what constitutes a room. Most times this is evident; other times a room may not be as obvious, espe-cially when considering open spaces of contemporary houses or loft apartments. The general rule of thumb is that a room is a room if it has an identifiable entry, be it a door, an opening, or archway.

If you have more than one door in a room, choose the one most often used as your main entry door; if you still are in doubt, use the largest entry. Of course, if you use the traditional method, you place the bagua stations according to the designated direction as explained in the chart on page 53.

Once you have designated the entry door to a room, position the bagua template so that the front or bottom part of the bagua is placed along the wall with the entry door. With this configuration, the main entry will fall either within the wisdom/knowledge, self/career, or the compassion/helpful people sector.

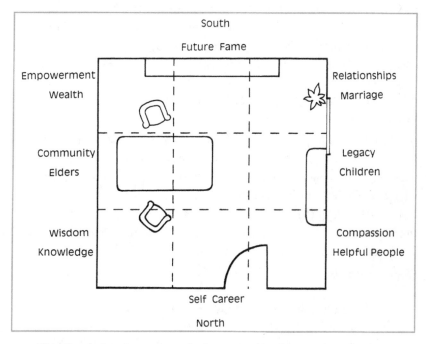

This illustration shows how the bagua is placed over a home office.

Frequently Asked Questions about the Bagua

Our workshop participants ask more questions about the bagua than any other feng shui topic. They see the bagua as something they can go home and immediately implement; however, they also understand that there are special considerations when applying the bagua over their house or room. Following is a list of some commonly asked questions along with the answers.

1. Half the time I enter my condo through the front door; other times I enter through the patio entrance. Which do I use as the entry door for the purpose of positioning the bagua?

In this case, use the front door to align the bagua. The front door holds more status and is considered as the main entry by the public. Since you frequently use the front door, it is the clear-cut winner in the entry door contest.

2. If my enclosed sunroom extends from the main part of the house, do I include it in the bagua?

Traditional feng shui teaches that an extension that is less than one-third of one side of the house where the extension occurs should not be included in the bagua grid. In fact, this small extension strengthens the bagua station to which it is attached. If the extension is more than one-third of one side of the house where the extension occurs, then you include it in the grid layout; this will cause a missing area of the bagua to occur and you need to correct the situation. Keep in mind that it is more important to apply the bagua over the sunroom itself.

3. Do I include my garage as part of the bagua?

Yes, although it is not an area where you spend a lot of time, keeping each area neat and clean goes a long way to improving your life. Also, that ton of stuff in your garage making it difficult to maneuver becomes just one more unneeded obstacle in your life.

4. What if I have an upstairs level?

You treat each floor separately and place a bagua grid over each level.

5. Can I place the bagua over my yard?

You bet your green thumb! It is advisable to place a separate bagua over the front yard and another over the back yard. If each yard has a separate entrance or threshold, even if implied, a bagua is needed.

6. Can I use the bagua at the office?

Talk about a powerful results-oriented tool. Yes, it is a must whether in a large corporate setting or an office in your home or apartment. Want to be superefficient? Place it over your desk.

7. What happens if there is a wall of windows taking up an entire bagua station?

The wall of windows can still be incorporated into your self-improvement theme by keeping those windows clean and free of cracks. Remember, dirt and cracked windows send a negative message that can prove counterproductive to your intentions.

8. My parents live in an apartment where the dining room and living room are divided by a hall and French doors that they always keep open. Should they analyze those two rooms together?

Treat each as a separate room because each room has an entrance. This is especially true in this case, since the rooms are separated by a hall.

9. I share an apartment with two other women. There is a living room, dining room, kitchen, and two bathrooms; each of us has our own bedroom. How would the bagua be used in our situation?

First of all, each of you can start with your own bedroom. After that, one suggestion might be to do one room as a collective effort so that is has meaning to all of you. We suggest the kitchen, since most people have similarly agreed upon symbols for the kitchen. Sit down with your roommates and discuss the other rooms; it may be that once they see you are knowledgeable on the subject, they will let you take the lead. If this is the case, make sure you are considerate of your roommates.

Chapter 6

Activating the Stations of Life

> "Every aspect of our environment carries symbolic meaning and has an effect on us whether we are aware of them or not."
>
> —Jennifer Dent

NOW THAT YOU HAVE a good understanding of the bagua, it is time to bring change to your environment and your life. By working the bagua, *you* are becoming an integral part of your life. You plan, participate, nurture yourself, ask for help, and help others. You challenge yourself and aspire to reach your dreams.

At this point you are ready to activate the stations. Use the bagua grid as a guide to help you place symbolic or sensorial enhancements such as artwork, prized possessions, family photos, furniture, aroma, light, and colorful objects in each room. Use a feature that connects your intention or wish with a specific sector of the bagua. For example, if you need help achieving a career objective, you might use a favorite business quote for an infusion of inspiration or a memento of a meaningful achievement to remind yourself that you've been able to reach goals in the past, and you can reach them again. These items would work well in the self/career and the future/fame sectors.

Your enhancers should be meaningful to you in that they inspire, motivate, and encourage you to take action or change behavior. With this in mind, the strength of the bagua lies in the strength of your symbols. Because it is important that you deeply and personally relate to your enhancers, use symbols *from your own* culture, belief system, and life experiences.

A Word about Symbolism

A phenomenon we often observe is that Americans interested in feng shui often buy Chinese objects to use as feng shui adornments or enhancements. Why is this? First of all, America is a young nation, and second, it is composed of a multitude of ethnic, racial, and religious groups; that's why it's called a melting pot. For these reasons, we have very few commonly held symbols. China, an ancient country, is composed of one ethnic/racial group and has very few religions. For these reasons, the Chinese have a multitude of commonly shared symbols for every imaginable situation. Take, for example, the popular Chinese prosperity symbol— a statue of a three-legged toad on top of coins. Americans who casually use this toad fail to understand that the symbolic association of this particular statue to wealth is historically embedded in the Chinese culture, folklore, and a commonly shared belief system.

China, India, and other ancient civilizations have images steeped in folklore, religion, and mythology. It would be highly unlikely that someone from Hong Kong would use a symbolic feature from another country or culture. Conversely, each person should use symbols from his or her own background, religion, culture, ethnic group, or belief system—this is how your environment starts to have meaning for you.

Every culture has its own unique myth and symbols; the use of Chinese items does not equate to effective feng shui if those items are of little significance to you. Following is a chart of protective symbols from various cultures. We invite you to add to this chart by adding your own symbol from your cultural, ethnic, or spiritual/religious background. Of course, you can always develop your own personal feature.

CULTURE	SYMBOL	PLACEMENT	DERIVATION
China	Bagua mirror	Outside, over front door	Chinese Taoist philosphy
India	Twin fish	Building entrance	Hindu mythology
Jewish	Mezuzah	Door post	Hebrew Bible
Greek	Evil eye plague	Inside, over door	Greek tradition

Although there are nine individual stations, they should be considered as part of an interconnected system and worked in conjunction with the other stations, *especially the opposite station.* Much like yin/yang, the opposite station brings completion and balance to the continuum. Areas opposite each other mutually support and bolster each other. For example, if you want to improve the relationships in your life, first you must know and improve yourself. The wisdom/knowledge area is opposite the relationship/marriage area. It is the wisdom/knowledge station that emphasizes our self-improvement through meditation, education, reading, or any other vehicle that helps you in your quest to become a better person. The more you better yourself, the more likely you will attract positive people. So, if it's romance you want, your chance of success is strengthened if you activate both the relationship/marriage and wisdom/knowledge areas.

Following we have listed each station in the bagua and the objects that tend to enhance that station, as well as those objects that tend to negate them. It is just as important to limit negative influences as it is to increase positive ones. We also bring in some traditional feng shui by mentioning the elements associated with each station.

Your Self/Career Station

The self/career area not only has to do with your career but also who you are as an individual and your chosen life path. Monetary success and prestige are not the true measure of your self-worth. How narrow it would be to define yourself only by your career, especially if you are stuck in a career either not of your choosing or liking. This area pertains to your personal "life mission" and should include the broad picture of whom and what you value in all areas of your life. It encourages the business executive to pursue a hidden desire to become a musician or a musician to become a business executive.

Your life can be defined as a journey. It is best to choose the direction of your path but not necessarily the outcome. Being open to the universe helps one keep an open mind to a multitude of life solutions instead of a few. It is therefore an area devoted to self-expression and the path you venture on to reach self-actualization, which includes your profession, career, or life mission. Think in terms of the present when you think of this area. The opposite station, future/fame, is what is in front of you, what you have to look forward to as you traverse your life path. Water is an appropriate element for this station, for it helps you flow *with* and not *against* your journey on the "river of life."

- **Objects:** Personal and meaningful items; pictures or paintings of nature scenes that contain gentle pathways or waterways that symbolize your journey through life; fountain or other Water features; area rug; adequate lighting to remind you of the here and now and to light your way to a bright future; plants or flowers; any item that welcomes those who enter; pleasant aromas; quotes or affirmations about living in the present; any item that symbolizes your personal life mission, including a meaningful career

- **Elements:** Water or Metal
- **Opposite station:** Future/fame
- **Negative objects:** Dim lighting, dangerous or slippery flooring, uninviting or unwelcoming due to lack of decorative features or because of clutter; no feature that welcomes those who enter

Your Wisdom/Knowledge Station

This area represents inner strength and personal growth. You not only acquire knowledge but also keep yourself open to receive wisdom, thus improving a strong sense of self. It's important to understand that knowledge has more to do with facts, while wisdom is about learning the lesson behind the facts.

Allowing quiet time for meditating and/or praying, reading, and writing are excellent yin activities, while attending a class, teaching, or reciting poetry would be great yang activities tied to this area of life. All are meant to further your desire to improve yourself. A good relationship with yourself can only enhance your relationships with others. Keep in mind that feng shui promotes a holistic approach to living, so the knowledge and wisdom needed is not only to improve the mind but also the spirit and the body.

- **Objects:** Books, bookshelves; rock garden; ceramic items or artwork depicting a landscape, mountains, animals/birds known for their solitary nature, such as an eagle; inspirational quotes or artwork depicting someone reading, meditating, praying, teaching/instructing, or of a higher power; a reading corner or meditation area; other items to use would be a lamp, lighting, floor pillows, desk or study table; this is the area of the bagua that can feature a solitary theme

- **Elements:** Earth and Fire
- **Opposite station:** Relationship
- **Negative Objects:** Symbols or mementos of other people's accomplishments; uncomfortable chair; poor lighting; piles of papers or books never used

Your Community/Elders Station

Your lineage, family, and community history are important because they all factor into who you are. Whether you have good or severed family ties, you need to acknowledge talents, gifts, and heritage bestowed upon you from those who have gone before you. Of course parents are the most obvious; however, aunts, uncles, or elders in general are to be included as well as communities that you come from, be it geographic, political, social, cultural, religious, ethnic, or business related. If you are part of such groups, they are part of your communities and the leaders of those groups are your elders (even if your pastor or spiritual leader is younger than you are!). This area concentrates on the gifts, talents, and wisdom bestowed on you by others who have gone before you or those that provide guidance, leadership, strength, and direction. This area also represents your support systems and networks.

- **Objects:** Healthy plants, flowers; water fountain; family photos, especially those containing older family members, people you admire, and those who came before you;

photos/books of sports figures, noted people from a particular field or cause; respected businesspeople such as founders or major contributors to a business, field of expertise, etc; family crest; tall furniture or tall architectural features; telephone and computer; awards or recognition for community service; artwork depicting trees, woods, etc., or water scenes; any symbol or inspirational quote that instills one with a sense of support or community; family heirlooms

- **Elements:** Wood and Water
- **Opposite station:** Legacy/children
- **Negative objects:** Artwork with a solitary theme; seating for one; items that are allowed to collect dust and dirt; quotations stressing the power of one

Your Empowerment/Wealth Station

This area has to do with how you are empowered in your life. The more empowered you are, the more you will achieve what is important and reach your full potential. Traditional feng shui refers to this as the wealth station; however, material wealth is but a small part in the definition of prosperity. In order to reach your full potential, you must be able to grow and change. You can immediately benefit from an attitude of abundance. Do this by recognizing the blessings that are presently in your life; releasing negative language, behavior, and attitudes; allowing yourself to envision your goals and aspirations; praying and meditating; and releasing your intentions to the universe.

- **Objects:** Objects associated with movement, such as wind, mobiles, or fans; healthy plants, including silk plants, artwork depicting wood scenes, plant life such as garden pictures; indoor fountain or fish tank (keep all Water features clean); lamp or light; comfortable chair or desk; awards, diplomas, or any items of recognition that inspire you; inspirational, spiritual, or motivational quotes; books that have a self-empowerment theme, such as books on spirituality, health, finance, etc.

- **Elements:** Wood and Water
- **Opposite station:** Compassion/helpful people
- **Negative objects:** Unhealthy plants; broken, cracked, or uncared-for items; barren-looking artwork such as a desert scene; piles of bills or uncompleted projects

Your Future/Fame Station

Your life is a journey and your future, although unknown, is always in front of you. A bright future comes from your convictions, talents, value system, and actions. If you are to incorporate the notion of fame and recognition, then it should encompass the way you want others to know the "real" you, not what is considered superficial. While it is important to be recognized by others, your opinion of yourself is more important.

This area should be used to bring about clarity and vision for your goals and aspirations. You need enlightenment, inspiration, and guidance. Strong doses of encouragement, validation, and support go a long way to help you bring about success in your life. It's fine to incorporate symbols of your past achievements and accomplishments, but don't go overboard; too many reminders of past victories might keep you living in the past. If you think about a bright future, the Fire element comes to mind. Like a fire, you need to shine.

- **Objects:** Lighting, lamps; clean objects such as windows, floors, etc.; candles, incense; lighthouse or artwork depicting

lighthouses; artwork that shows anything rising up, like hot-air balloons, kites, or birds flying; artwork or quotations depicting your dreams and aspirations; mementos of achievements or meaningful awards; pyramid or triangular-shaped objects; animals, animal prints or photos; leather items or leather furniture; plants
- **Elements:** Fire and Wood
- **Opposite station:** Self/career
- **Negative Objects:** Overdisplaying of past achievements; books that make fun of or belittle anyone; artwork that depicts rain or storms; clutter, especially on top of shelves; seating that appears weak

Your Relationships/Marriage Station

This station has to do, primarily, with all meaningful relationships, whether they are romantic, relationships with peers or business associates, or relationships with friends. Since there are specific stations for children and communities, including family, keep the focus on romance, friendship, or peer/business relationships. This station should promote being open, flexible, receptive, and making room for others. Some people have no problem with intimacy while others put up barriers, which are usually exhibited in their living spaces. When we find someone who does not want to follow through with suggestions or corrections to the relationship area, we are usually dealing with someone who is resistant to becoming intimately involved. Having healthy and intimate relationships with others strengthens you by forming connections to people who can significantly contribute to the quality of your life. Many of us have lessened our connection to nature, people, the universe, and our higher power or spirit.

Strengthening our relationships keeps us from becoming self-absorbed, lonely, isolated, and inflexible.

Whether you are wishing to bring about a romance, strengthen a business relationship, or develop a friendship, it is important to remember that relationships are reciprocal; you must be willing to give and take. If you are inflexible and not willing to change, you are creating overwhelming, self-imposed obstacles. Likewise, you should not just accept the next person who comes along; give some thought to what qualities you want in a person.

- **Objects:** Any symbols or items that represent a strong, healthy, and loving relationship. For couples: use pairs (for example, a picture of two lovebirds, two lovers, hearts, symbols of love, or two or more friends); posters, paintings, and photos of you and your significant other, such as vacation or wedding photos. For friendships: use artwork showing groups of people or animals; quotes or affirmations pertaining to love or meaningful relationships; intimate seating arrangement, seats with cushions; photos of close friends. For business/peer partnerships or office teams: use appropriate business symbols that fortify the team such as the company logo or mission statement; any item that symbolizes a relationship to you; any artwork depicting earth landscapes that look lush, containing two or more people/animals; throws, pillows or stuffed animals; seating for two or more; lush plant or flower arrangements; empty space in a drawer or closet
- **Elements:** Earth and Fire
- **Opposite station:** Wisdom/Knowledge
- **Negative objects:** Absence of photos of loved ones or friends; a screen or divider; piles of work to be done; artwork

depicting a solitary person; large trash cans, dirt, and cob-webs; clocks or any mechanical items that don't work

Your Legacy/ Children Station

This area represents your legacy, not only through your descen-dants who represent your physical creation, but also in expressions of your creativity, imagination, or special talents or gifts.

Nothing invigorates creativity like the senses. You interpret your environment through your senses, so the more you awaken the senses, the more alive your world becomes—creativity soars. Just as you give birth to children, you also give birth to other cre-ations such as art, music, a favorite food entrée, a poem, or busi-ness idea. It is easy to see how this area has to do with creativity. What you create—what you leave behind—says to the world: "This is the valuable contribution I leave the universe." For some it might be their artwork, representations of musical instruments that a person plays, mementos from one's profession, or objects of a hobby. More traditionally, representations of our children are used. Keeping in mind the importance of the child within, this should be a fun area.

- **Objects:** Metal objects or artwork; jewelry; a decorative or seasonal arrangement; items that appeal to the senses; musical equipment/instruments; artwork depicting chil-dren playing; favorite hobby item or photo of such item; pictures of children (your own, nieces/nephews, or other children you have an attachment to); supplies used for cre-ative activity; fun, unusual, or unique artwork or objects; quotations or sayings involving kids or creativity; mean-ingful childhood items; photo albums, game area; lamp or lights; plants

- **Elements:** Metal and Earth
- **Opposite station:** Community/elders
- **Negative objects:** Serious quotations; books of rules and regulations; an overemphasis on yourself; important house-hold records; emptiness; clutter among important items; poor lighting

Your Compassion/Helpful People Station

Traditionally this area represents heaven and the bounty bestowed upon you, usually in the form of helpful people and their support, compassion, guidance, and love. You are not meant to find all of the answers yourself—the help of others multiplies the power of one. Allow others to mentor, guide, support, and love; the rewards are infinite. Be open and receptive.

A more contemporary perspective expands the definition of helpful people by adding "compassion" to this station, reminding you of the importance of reciprocity—if you expect helpful people to enter your life then you, too, must be helpful and compassionate to others. Think of a volunteer activity; take time to listen to someone in need; teach a child to read. Interdependency is the ultimate goal of this station—you begin to understand healthy ways that you can help others and how others can help you. We collectively improve the world we inhabit.

- **Objects:** Table for placing objects; place to sit down; any accessories that are signs of hospitality, such as a coat closet, place for keys, or umbrella stand; lamp or spot-light; trash can; pictures of people in helping situations, helpful people or mentors, teachers, clients, customers, etc., you've had in your life; artwork of spiritual guides,

saints, angels, etc.; quotations, affirmations, or sayings relating to spiritual guidance or compassion; items you relate to on a spiritual or religious level; telephone and address book; round bowls; metal objects; meaningful objects or tokens of gratitude received from those you have helped
- **Elements:** Metal and Earth
- **Opposite station:** Empowerment/wealth
- **Negative objects:** No room on tabletops for personal belongings; stuffed coat closets; bad lighting; any artwork, books, or quotations that express a do-it-yourself attitude or theme; messy entrances

Your Health—Mind, Body, Spirit

The health area is the center, which directly corresponds to you, the individual, and as part of a community. The center represents gravity—your foundation. The surrounding eight stations, if fully activated, help you achieve health in mind, body, and spirit.

- **Objects:** Family seating area, well-kept and clean floor surfaces or rugs; good lighting; anything in middle of room should be clean and healthy looking; plants; water fountain
- **Element:** Earth and Fire
- **Negative objects:** Dirt, grime, or clutter; any furniture that looks uncomfortable or fragile; any items broken or cracked

Scents for the Bagua

Aromatherapy is a very effective bagua enhancement. Incense, diffusers, potpourris, or sprays can be utilized. As far as aromas are concerned, a little goes a long way, so keep exposure brief. Here is a scent for each sector:

Self/career: Lemon—helps eliminate indecisiveness

Wisdom/knowledge: Rosemary—good for memory, perception, and helps balance mind/body

Community/elders: Orange—helps one feel adaptable, warm, and less self-conscious

Empowerment/wealth: Neroli—counters fear and lack of confidence, and redirects energy in positive way

Future/fame: Mint—uplifting, counters mental fogginess and helps with focus

Relationships/marriage: Rose—stirs romance; good for healing relationship turmoil

Legacy/children: Grapefruit—revives and lightens; good for "inner child" work

Compassion/helpful people: Jasmine—reduces apathy and indifference; bolsters harmony

Health: Sage—reduces nervousness, grief, physical exhaustion, and insomnia; encourages introspection and stimulates the senses

A Few Final Words

Now that we have explained the bagua, you might be eager to paint, redecorate, or buy the "right" symbol. Although a certain something or other may call your name as you pass it in the store, it is far better to start with what you have. You may discover that the small collection of teacups that your grandmother gave you is ideal for the community/elders area; or you may have books about nutrition, money management, and business networking that would fit quite nicely on the shelves in your empowerment/wealth area.

To relieve any anxiety about using the bagua in your personal space, we offer the following advice:

1. Take your time.
2. Be creative with your symbols/objects.
3. Change your enhancements from time to time.
4. Keep it simple.
5. Tie your intention to your symbols.
6. Share what you are doing with one supportive person
7. Pay attention to changes as they occur; better yet, keep a journal.
8. Try using nontangible activators such as aromas or music (refer to the book *The Mozart Effect* by Don Campbell).
9. Have fun.
10. Use what you have.

Section II
How to Evaluate What You Have

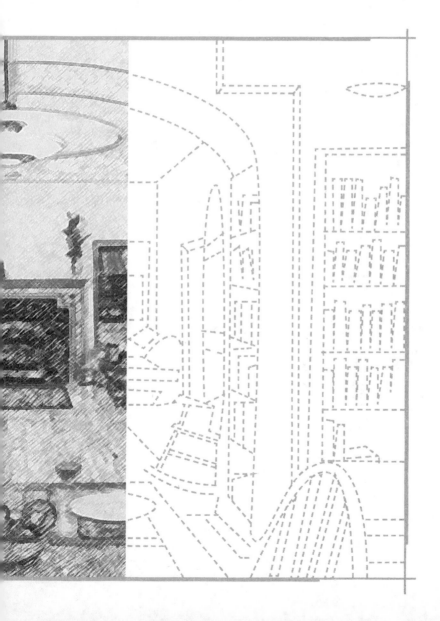

Chapter 7

Get a Good Look at What You Have

> "People who are satisfied appreciate what they have in life and don't worry about how it compares to what others have. Valuing what you have over what you do not or cannot have leads to greater happiness."
>
> —David Niven, Ph.D.

BEFORE YOU WAVE YOUR feng shui magic wand, you must put on your "feng shui eyes." This will provide you with an objective way to look at your physical environment to see if it really does support and nurture you. Feng shui eyes don't develop overnight—but not to worry. With some guidance, simple exercises, and an evaluation process, you will develop a vision that will help you create an environment in ways you never imagined. Even if you are renting a furnished apartment and your lease has a lot of "don'ts" and very few "do's," you still have the power to realize a space that supports you in all areas of your life.

Remember this: When you change your environment, *you* make things happen. You begin to take a proactive approach to creating not only a more livable and friendly space, but also a more empowering one.

This is what your "feng shui eyes" will enable you to do:

- Scope your living area for hidden messages
- Evaluate what you have in light of being an asset to reaching your goals
- Toughen up in order to pare away what might be harmful to you
- Incorporate colors for emotional response
- Understand both the nature and function of each room
- Make choices that support your best and highest self

Playing Detective

Although it is always a good idea to evaluate your space, remember that the reason you are doing this intensive study of your "digs" is for the express purpose of realizing your three wishes. You may prefer to call them aspirations, intentions, or goals. Many of our clients tell us that they want to bring romance into their lives; others want to start anew after a divorce; some are looking to improve their career situation.

As feng shui professionals, we are trained to scope a client's surroundings for the purpose of unraveling an unspoken story. Feng shui is the language of the environment, speaking loud and clear to those trained to interpret its tale. Coupled with detailed information that the client shares about his or her personal or business life, we are able to expose an intricate chronicle that enables us to help the client achieve her or his intentions and goals and eliminate negative patterns and actions.

In order to be a detective in your own space, you first need to figure out what in your environment is working for or against you. Here are some pertinent questions to ask:

- What is my environment saying about me?
- Does my living or working space support or sabotage my best efforts to attain health, happiness, and abundance in all areas of my life?

Our visualization exercise will help you answer these questions:

Sit quietly and close your eyes; keep them closed throughout this exercise. Travel to the room in your home where you spend the most time. Think of one of your three wishes and ask yourself: Does this space support my current self-improvement endeavor?

Without thinking about it, you will know whether your environment is mirroring your best and positive self, whether it is supportive or destructive, and whether clutter is fostering procrastination. You may find that the bulging shoebox that contains unpaid bills and important financial papers sitting in plain view in your home office is doing nothing to further your desire to improve your financial situation.

Now the next step is to follow a plan of action that will help you read your home, apartment, or office, following its lead in formulating a prescription for healing your space. Keeping in the detective mode, start to focus your feng shui eyes on certain locations and features within your existing space. It is recommended that you record your observations or take pictures. Here are some hot spots to observe.

Thresholds

Entrances to your home or apartment are extremely important because they represent the transition between the outside, active world into your place of safe haven. Thresholds also welcome guests and make your first impression on visitors. Are they clean, uncluttered, and well lit? Are there welcoming features such as plants, a fountain, or a welcome mat? Also keep in mind that all entrances that lead into your dwelling need examining especially if others in your household use an entrance different from the one you use.

Pathways

Paths are important, as they create the feeling of flow and movement. Check to see if you are stepping over or around furniture or stacks of clutter. Obstacles in your physical environment mirror obstacles in your life.

View of Nature

Our affinity with nature is inbred. One of the most beneficial feng shui cures for so much of what ails us is to allow a view of nature to enter. Are your drapes closed? Is your furniture positioned to take advantage of a beautiful vista? Hint: If you live in an apartment where such a view isn't possible, it becomes more important to bring in prints or paintings of nature scenes.

Clutter

One of the most damaging factors in your environment is also one of the easiest to remedy. Clutter is relative. What constitutes clutter for one person may not be to another. If you are naturally neat and orderly, an accessory out of place is clutter. If you are like the rest of us, clutter means stacks of paper and stuffed closets. At this point, check to see where your clutter traps are and what they consist of. An entire chapter will thoroughly address the topic later on, so the only thing you need to do at this point is check to see where your clutter traps are and what they consist of.

Broken Items or Items That Don't Work

Feng shui is a metaphor for living. Anything that remains broken or out of order is sending a negative message.

Color

One of the most effective ways to bring about positive emotional and behavioral change is with color. Even if you can't paint due to restrictions, there are other ways to bring in color. Tablecloths, napkins, pillows, throws, drapes, etc., are all easy and quick color vehicles. Become aware of the colors in your space. Are you using the same color over and over? Are you using an inappropriate color in your bedroom? See the following table for a list of colors and the emotional impact of each.

COLOR	EFFECTS	BE CAREFUL
Blue	Soothes and relaxes Expresses uniqueness Decreases the appetite Brings attention to needs of the individual	Too much blue can be depressing Not a good color for an activity room
Red	Stimulates and motivates Increases the appetite Use sparingly to invite romance Seems exciting Invites action	Too much red can agitate or anger Not a good color for rooms of solitude, such as a library, or for rooms of rest
Orange	Warm and welcoming Promotes interaction and conversation Also increases the appetite Supports common goals of group Peach is a good color for gathering rooms	Too much orange can make one feel anxious Not a good color when focus and concentration are needed Certain shades can appear cheap

COLOR	EFFECTS	BE CAREFUL
Yellow	Promotes cheerfulness, hope Good for focus and intellectual pursuits Encourages compassion and understanding Good color for kitchens	Too much yellow can make people nervous, especially children Not a good color to use in bathrooms or in a room for meditation
Green	Soothing, healing, and peaceful Good color for creativity Represents new beginnings, change Can be warming or cooling depending on shade	Too much olive green can seem depressing or dingy Makes food appear appetizing; good plate color for finicky eaters Stay away from green if you want to maintain status quo Color associated with envy
Purple	Color of spirituality Emphasizes the individual Lighter shades with splashes of true purple good for preteen and teenage girls' bedrooms Lends to higher consciousness and creativity	Refrain from using purple in rooms for group activity Can appear pretentious
Brown	Represents stability, security, and groundedness Maintains the status quo Tan and beige are good colors to use in rooms involving family interaction	Brown should not be used on a large scale in a room, as it can seem muddy Do not use brown where change is desired Brown can thwart vitality
Black	Seen as sophisticated Adds mystery Considered a power color Good as an accent color to accentuate or bring attention to	Refrain from using black in large quantities, as it can depress Black slows down activity

COLOR	EFFECTS	BE CAREFUL
White	Signifies cleanliness and order Use to showcase anything you want to display Makes rooms appear larger and taller Good color for kitchen and bathroom Good room color for interviews	Too much white in a room will make people feel "on display" Not an intimate color Can create glare and eye strain—use off-white instead

Start Your Evaluation Process

Your feng shui eyes should now be activated, making you more objective about the decisions you make regarding the changes in your home. Realize that the longer you live in a place, the more accustomed to your surroundings you become and the more oblivious you are to negative features. We hear the statement "I never saw *that* until you pointed it out" from our clients on a regular basis.

One such consultation involved Ana, a kitchen and bath designer, who complained of workaholic tendencies. Being self-employed, she never knew when to call it quits. Long hours spent at the office and with customers were followed by still more hours when she arrived home. Upon touring her home we saw a large collection of hummingbird paintings and statues, which she'd had for more than ten years. When we pointed out that these birds were perpetual motion machines, she immediately understood how they mirrored and reinforced her work behavior. Obvious as it was to us, she had put up her blinders. As a result of the consultation, Ana decided to keep a few favorite hummingbirds and gave away or sold the others.

It is not unusual for a person to stop noticing what is around them—to stop being aware of the broken clock, the cracked window, or the bookshelves packed to the gill. You start getting comfy, cozy with environmental features that harm rather than heal and that deplete rather than support. Developing your feng shui eyes will help you break this negative behavior and allow you to start understanding the connections between you and your environment.

Now you have come to the turning point. You have learned the feng shui basics of connectedness, chi, yin/yang, the five elements, and the bagua. Your newly acquired feng shui eyes complete your feng shui tool kit. With your newly developed skills, knowledge, and heightened awareness about your surroundings, you are now ready to take action. This is the beginning of bringing about positive change in your life by creating an environment that supports your dreams, intentions, and goals.

These are the components of your feng shui tool kit:

1. Three wishes
2. List of important connections (What and who are important to you. What is significant to you may include nature, the world you inhabit, country, community, work/business, and activities. Who is significant may include your higher power, family, friends, peers, pets, and other loved ones. Living in the Tao means following the ways of nature and connecting with the world around you.)
3. Understanding of yin/yang (refer to Chapter 2 for charts and suggestions).
4. Understanding of the five elements (refer to Chapter 3 for charts and suggestions).
5. Understanding of the bagua (refer to Chapters 5 and 6 for explanations and suggestions).
6. Your "feng shui eyes"

Getting Out of Your Own Way

Here you are, ready to start one of the most challenging, yet exciting, adventures you have ever embarked upon. Even though you are in your own space, consider this as new territory. Be careful: There may be traps all around you that could hinder you in your task of objectively evaluating your surroundings. It is essential that you recognize what could confront you as you take your journey. Beware of these roadblocks.

Tunnel Vision

Once you have lived in a space for so long, you stop seeing the obvious, which might be clutter, inappropriate artwork, elements that are not balanced, colors that create tension, too much yin, etc. Just imagine wearing blinders and you will easily understand how you might not see what is right in front of you.

Rationalization

We once recommended that a client remove a painting of a leopard that hung over her bed as it might send the wrong message to new suitors. "It shows that I am a strong woman" was her comeback. After we gently reminded her that she had already confided that most men seemed intimidated by her, she got the message and replaced the leopard painting with a print of *The Kiss*. If you can convince yourself that what is bad for you is really good, you just earned high marks in Rationalization 101. Take heart; it is human nature to rationalize. How else do you justify cabinets full of jelly jars that might serve a useful purpose someday or keeping seven pair of black shoes that you haven't worn in two years because basic black is essential for your wardrobe?

Keeping Something Because You Feel Obligated

This usually happens when you receive furniture or a gift from a friend or relative. Please don't think we are suggesting all such items have to go. Family heirlooms and keepsakes help keep us connected to our legacy and our roots; however, some furniture or decorative items just don't work. If this is the case, release yourself from their bonds and say bye-bye. You can give them to someone who may be able to use them or you might sell them, allowing you to purchase more appropriate articles.

Forgetting to Appreciate What You Have

Can't decide whether to keep the bedside tables that your mother gave you? Maybe a change in attitude will make the difference. Stop seeing them as hand-me-downs and start appreciating the history connected with them. If they look dingy, then polish or restore them. Be like Joyce, a client who decided to stop complaining about an unsightly coffee table and instead uncovered a unique treasure when she removed the dark and soiled wax buildup. This small act resulted in praise from her children about "mom's talents" and numerous offers from friends to buy what she once considered junk. The act of restoring the table also helped instill some much needed self-esteem to this recent divorcée.

If you are having trouble with any of these roadblocks, you might want to ask a friend to help you critique your space. Honest, objective feedback goes a long way in assessing your environment. Don't forget, taking inventory has to do with what you have on hand, not what is necessarily in sight. Dig into those closets, drawers, and storage units and start uncovering items that either support or hinder you. Trash or treasure—it's a keeper or a goner.

Chapter 8

Taking Inventory

> "I have seen people manage to create rooms that are indisputably charming and memorable, with almost no money and a generally undistinguished miscellany of possessions. This is what is meant by a sense of style."
>
> —Mary Gilliatt

LET'S TAKE INVENTORY in order to assess your living space. This activity is necessary so you can spot what's right, correct what's wrong, and find out what you have on hand. If you don't know what you already have on hand, it will be difficult to make the needed changes. Compare this activity to trying a new recipe and having to check for the necessary ingredients or assembling a shelving unit and looking for the correct tools to accomplish it. The benefit of doing this is that you save time and eliminate procrastination. We don't want you to delay activities or abandon your journey altogether.

Identifying what you have to work with helps you get the ball rolling. You start seeing immediate solutions to problems as you encounter them. This is what enabled Belinda, a client, to find a more appropriate item for her compassion/helpful people corner. After she removed a photo of a dead tree showing exposed roots that hung in this area, Belinda looked for and found a quotation in her "favorite quotes" file that she keeps on her computer. Originally these quotes were on small pieces of paper stuffed in her bedroom dresser drawer. At our suggestion, she recently stored them in a Microsoft Word file.

The quotation read: "O you who sit in the gardens, My companions are listening for your voice—Let me hear it!" (Solomon 8:13). After printing the quote on ivory stationery, she framed it in the same frame that was used for the tree photo. This was a quick solution at no cost that Belinda used to make a positive change.

Now that you know your mission for this chapter, make four trips around your dwelling in order to do the following: discover what you have on hand; assess your space through your five senses; evaluate the negative and positive aspects of your artwork and accessories; and determine how easy or difficult it is to move through your living space.

Before you start taking inventory, do a quick, preliminary decluttering excursion through your home or apartment: Find twenty-five items that, without a second thought, can immediately be thrown away. This might include old magazines and newspapers, chipped plates, old toiletries, expired prescriptions, rusted kitchen utensils, coats that don't fit, worn-out boots or shoes, inexpensive small appliances with faulty or frayed plugs or wiring (dangerous and not worth repairing), manuals for equipment you no longer own, old receipts, and items that are permanently out of order. If you thin out some junk, it is easier to concentrate on the treasures that you have.

Trip One—Going on a Scavenger Hunt

Many clients think we are going to ask them to spend a lot of money in order to implement the feng shui cures we recommend. To their relief, they already possess most of what they need. Some are very creative and have a knack for making something out of nothing. For example, Alise, who couldn't afford to buy wall covering, made a stencil by cutting a circular swirl pattern on a potato cut in half. Using some leftover soft green paint, she stenciled her dining room walls creating a faux-papered finish. Doing this brought much-needed movement (yang) to a room that was too quiet and still (too yin).

Other clients find that what doesn't work in one room is the magical missing ingredient for another room. For example, Gigi and Ben, married for four years, had tried unsuccessfully to get pregnant. We suggested adding some spice to their dull, beige bedroom by bringing in the Fire element (Fire is the element of passion and love). We grabbed the red cotton twin-size throw that was in the guest room, folded it, and placed it at the foot of their bed. The other Fire cure came about when Ben thought of a candle arrangement they received for their anniversary. To make a long story short, Gigi was pregnant in thirty days.

What do you have on hand? Let's find out by going on a scavenger hunt. Make this pursuit worthwhile by keeping your three wishes in mind; it's easier to spot the appropriate items.

A word of caution before you begin: Working with what you have should not be an excuse to keep clutter. There's a difference between keeping a faded light plate that can be covered with wallpaper and keeping a cracked light plate that you will never use.

Following is a list of items that might be found in many American households:

- Artwork (more on this in a following section)
- Throws or large pieces of fabric that can be used as a throw; fabric used to make slip covers, to cover pillows, to use as window treatments, or to use as a tablecloth
- Tablecloths that can be used as you would fabric, along with

napkins—both good to use to bring in color when painting is not possible

- Sheets that can be used as fabric or as wall covering
- Objects that can be re-covered, such as pillows, lamp shades, boxes, containers, cartons, frames, headboards, etc.
- Coffee and end tables with glass that have marred or scratched tops, and can be covered with wall covering, fabric, or a sheet cut to size and covered with glass
- Smaller pieces of fabric, wall covering, wrapping paper, or tissue paper—good for covering a number of small items such as boxes, cartons, light plates
- Tassels, fringe, cording, bells
- Calendars, post cards, photos
- Scarves—good to re-cover dingy lamp shades, pillows, or cover TVs when not in use
- Yard items, such as clay pots, birdhouses, yard art used as decorative items—good way to bring in reminders of out-doors
- Plants, flowers (live or silk); refrain from using dried flowers
- Mobiles or any items that can be used as a decorative hanging
- Empty birdcage—to use for candle display (use plate on bottom of cage)
- String, fishing line, twine, thin rope, hooks, curtain rods—use to hang a sheet or fabric when you need to separate one area into two, to create a private area or to hide electrical equipment
- Large plates and platters that can be used as part of a centerpiece
- Candles or tapers
- Shells, conchs, or other items collected from the beach

- Rocks, quartz, crystals, marbles, decorative tiles, ceramics, stoneware
- Leftover paint, brushes, stencils, or art supplies
- Various nature items such as gourds, evergreen branches, palm leaves, tall grass, flowers, driftwood, leaves, willow branches, etc.
- Various food items that can be used as part of centerpiece, such as lemons, oranges, asparagus, nuts, dill, peppers

Trip Two—Using All Your Senses

As humans, we interpret our environment through our senses. The more developed our senses are, the more we tune in to our surroundings. On this second trip use not only your eyes, but engage all of your senses. Awaken your senses and you unlock a new universe; keep your senses dormant and you become an outsider in your own home.

So, get ready to smell, see, touch, hear, and taste. Seek out objects, accessories, artwork, and such that evoke strong emotions both positively and negatively. Specifically, pay attention to what impacts you negatively. How to positively activate the senses is discussed in following chapters throughout the book. Use the following list to evaluate the negative.

- **What you see:** threatening, gloomy art; colors that depress, anger, or confuse; clutter that blocks and stagnates; electrical wiring from your computer or other appliances; too much light or darkness; sharp lines or edges; TV on for no reason; unhealthy plants; cracked or chipped items; broken glass or windows; leaky faucets. Even though all the senses are important, sight impacts human experience more than any of the other senses. About 70 percent of a person's sense receptors are located in the eyes.

The sense of sight is the main thoroughfare through which you judge, evaluate and understand your environment. Vision involves logic, meaning that you, the observer, must think about and form an opinion of what you see.

• **What you hear:** annoying noises; violence from the TV; negative talk; irritating music; too many sounds going on at the same time; hum of electrical appliances or lighting; loud traffic or construction noise.

The sense of hearing holds unbelievable power to heal the human body. Research has shown that various types of sounds such as music, drumming, the human voice, birds chirping and singing, and ocean waves splashing on the shore all work like acupuncture without needles, healing the body and emotions. Likewise, if the sounds in your environment cause you to react negatively and you are exposed to them regularly, imagine the damage your well-being is sustaining.

• **What you smell:** musty, damp, or foul odors; pet urine or the litterbox; aromas that trigger negative emotions; overpowering "pleasant aromas"—proof that too much of a good thing can be bad. The sense of smell is the only sense that evokes a purely emotional response.

A person's response to smell takes place within ten seconds after exposure; there is no thought process involved. For this reason, if a person smells a dirty litter box upon entering an apartment, his or her experience of the visit is tainted before it begins.

• **What you touch:** textures; *a lack* of tactile features; sharp edges; overabundance of hard surfaces, such as hardwood floors, wood furniture, glass-top tables without texture; not being able to touch what is alive, such as a pet, a person, a plant; not being able to feel a breeze from a window or fan, or the movement of running water, or touch a mobile to make it move.

Remember, you don't have to have physical contact in order to experience touch; a person can experience the texture of a luxurious piece of velvet fabric by just looking at it. Conversely, imagine seeing stark hard surfaces of table tops without any textural relief; how inviting is that?

• **What you taste:** Taste is the most intimate of all the senses because you have to experience it up close. No need to scope your space for negative aspects related to this sense. Rather, it is important for you to know how the presence of food or the act of eating can contribute significantly to your experience of place.

EXPERIENCING TASTE	TIP
Taste and smell are intricately related	If you want your child to partake of the bowl of apples sitting on the kitchen table, infuse a whiff of the corresponding aroma
Food is associated with hospitality	Place a bowl of individually wrapped candy in the entrance of your home or apartment
Various cultures, as evidenced by their literature, link food and sex	To heighten a romantic bedroom rendezvous, share food that oozes, is juicy, hot, and steamy, or is considered sumptuous, such as chocolate

Trip Three—Assessing Your Artwork

Ideally, art found in your home expresses your individual taste, culture, and personality. These art objects may include paintings, prints, photographs, murals, needlepoint, weavings, fabric art, collages, carved items, statues, metalwork, wall hangings, plates, vases, ceramics, calendars, wind chimes, mobiles, birdhouses, dollhouses, fountains, framed collectibles, religious items, fans, and other items.

Sometimes you might display art and objects given to you by others that don't reflect what you like. Someone may have absent-mindedly, or on purpose, left artwork or a collection behind due to a

divorce or loosing a roommate. As a result you may respond negatively each time you connect with these items visually or otherwise.

Your mission in this chapter is threefold: 1) Find art that supports and nurtures your dreams, aspirations, and goals; 2) eliminate pieces that depress, threaten, and convey a message contrary
to your dreams, aspirations, and goals; and 3) examine the placement of each piece you choose to keep. Make sure that where it is
placed achieves the desired effect or is an appropriate item for one
of the bagua sectors.

Here are some general guidelines for assessing artwork. Art
that depicts the following concepts and motifs tend to be the best
choices:

- Plants, flowers, and any healthy looking vegetation
- Nature, including landscapes, seascapes, gentle water scenes,
  fields of flowers, rolling mountains, and so on
- Favorite vacation spots
- Family or friends
- People in positive situations, such as interacting, dancing,
  reading, playing, embracing, walking, relaxing, and so on
- Hobbies, interests, or talents
- Nonthreatening wildlife and friendly animals
- Religious or spiritual icons, symbols, or entities
- Images with cultural or ethnic significance that relate to
  your own roots
- Motivational or inspirational quotations
- Family crests or mementos
- Meaningful or significant buildings or landmarks
- Seasonal or holiday related motifs

Art that depicts the following concepts and motifs should be
used with caution, and may be best eliminated. In any case, be very

careful where you place these pieces in your living space or within any of the bagua stations:

- Art that depicts sadness, depression, aggression, or gloom
- Threatening nature scenes
- Dying or wilted vegetation
- People in dangerous situations, such as sitting on the edge of a cliff or a weapon pointed at a person
- Predatory wild animals used as a focal point in a public area
- Sharp, angular features or tangent lines
- Weapons or war scenes except in a special collection display area and limited in size
- Cracked or split people and/or body parts
- Demonic or scary scenes, creatures, or entities
- Replicas of statues with heads or limbs missing
- A person breathing fire
- Warships or other battlefield scenes, especially in a bedroom or family room
- A print or photograph depicting a solitary person as a focal point in a gathering room or in the relationship sector of the bagua

Although we warn against using certain types of art, there are always exceptions. We once consulted for a couple that wanted us to prepare their home for sale. As we entered their home, a large painting of a Bengal tiger greeted us from a very prominent position in the foyer. Momentarily frozen in our tracks, we were more startled than welcomed. On our advice, they removed the painting from the foyer, replacing it with a beautiful painting of flowers in a vase. This made the entrance much more welcoming to visitors and potential buyers.

Because the tiger painting was a family favorite, it didn't make sense to dispose of it. What was inappropriate in the entrance became the ideal enhancement when placed in the husband's private office behind his desk. This strong animal made him feel motivated and empowered as he entered his space. Since it was behind him, it was not a disturbance while he performed his paperwork duties.

Threatening animals can be acceptable in an entryway if they are small. Some Chinese families, for example, display small statues of threatening animals in their entrances. It is a gentle way of letting guests know that, although they are welcome, their behavior is being observed.

Your art rendezvous will not be a quick pass around your home. Just as you might need to remove what is not working for you, you also need to find items to take the place of what you have removed. Sometimes you can move a few things to a different location. But even if you need new art, you may be able to create that with materials you already have, with a little creativity. For example:

- Two or more calendar pictures can be mounted on white or painted cardboard or framed and hung to create an attractive grouping.
- Fabric or wallpaper can be glued to any hard surface, such as cardboard, particle board, or wood. If you do this, wrap the edges or frame the covered board.
- Items from the outdoors such as pressed leaves or flowers, pine twigs or cones, sprigs of berry, palm branches, and cattails can be mounted on a hard surface that has been covered with some fabric or framed under glass.
- Centerpieces can be made from items found throughout your home, including the kitchen. Start to imagine what masterpiece could be created by using fruit, napkins, plates,

leftover wrapping ribbon, scraps of fabric, candles, rocks, baskets, ceramic planters, leftover silk flowers—and the list goes on.

If you do get rid of any pieces of art, keep the frames for your new pieces.

✳ Client Story: Nature's Solutions at No Cost

The cashier said, "That will be $129.80." Gayle had selected materials at a local craft store for two winter decorative planters to place on each side of her front door. After recovering from sticker shock, she decided against the purchase. She returned home, where she decided to browse the "aisles" of her back yard, basement, and kitchen for appropriate items. Using two large, straw baskets as containers, she created what we would call *nature masterpieces* using pine tree branches, pine cones, pomegranates, a few red glass tree ornaments, red and white decorative cloth ribbon, and some silk berry branches. What resulted were entrance centerpieces that rivaled those found in a Neiman Marcus catalog. A little creativity, resourcefulness, recycling, and inspiration from nature proved to be ingredients for a win-win solution.

Trip Four—Going with the Flow: The Importance of Movement

How easy is it for you to move from the exterior of your dwelling to the interior? How do you move about from one room to another? How easy is it to maneuver while you are within a room? As you give some thought to these questions, imagine that you have invited a first-time guest to your home. Try putting yourself in that person's shoes; it might be easier for you to honestly answer those questions. If a person:

- Struggles to find your front door
- Pushes an out of order doorbell
- Is greeted by a broom and dustpan as he or she enters the entrance
- Comes to a standstill because the path to the living room is cluttered

. . . then you have problems.

Gentle movement throughout your home is a sign of a healthy space, and that's not just our opinion. Traditional Chinese medicine (TCM) supports this premise. According to TCM, one sign of good health is unobstructed flow of fluids, air, and food throughout the body. If this flow, which is described as chi, is blocked, moves too fast, or becomes stagnant, disharmony and imbalance occur. When this happens, a person is considered sick and unhealthy.

According to TCM, the external movement and flow that surrounds a person in their environment also influences internal movement and flow within a person's body. Chinese medicine does not distinguish between the two but instead views both as part of an interrelated whole.

Take a look at your pathways, including sidewalks, garden paths, halls, and stairways. Observe how you move from room to room as well as through a room. Be on the lookout for:

- Straight, fast-moving paths
- Blocked lanes
- Furniture that blocks an entrance to another room
- Overcrowded areas

All these conditions can be fixed at no cost to you. Soften a straight hallway by hanging items on the walls or placing them on the floor in an alternating pattern; avoid placing objects directly opposite each other. You can bring out that collection of post cards and create a collage of your favorite travel spots or hang alternating sconces. Try filling them with some silk plants. Halls are great places to hang family photos or a collection of framed prints.

Unblock lanes by removing what is in the way. This may sound simpler than it is; some people find halls and stairways convenient dumping grounds. Tackle these areas and resolve not to create these blockages again. Halls and stairs represent paths in your life; do yourself a favor by keeping them free of obstacles. Find it difficult to keep these areas clear of your piles? Keep a basket at the bottom of the stairs and carry it up with you when it is full. Find a convenient spot in a hall for another basket and empty it whenever it gets full. Just remember, the basket's contents become clutter if they remain in it for more than three weeks.

Practicality is important, so make a place for those snowy shoes, boots, or sand-filled tennis shoes by placing a small shoe rack (for a family) or small area rug by a side or back entrance door. If you are an apartment dweller with only one entry door, use a place mat there for a pair of shoes or boots. It is always best to place shoes to the left side of the door. Humans gravitate to the right upon entering a space, so keep what is unsightly to the left side if possible. Be careful; don't let this become an area where footwear accumulates.

Next, consider anything that interferes with moving from one room to another, anything that forces people to squeeze through a space that should be open. Here is a hint: Observe first-time guests as they walk through your rooms and notice if they bump into or have to go out of their way to move in and out of your spaces. As a solution, remove the culprit piece of furniture or place it in another room.

Now you are ready to resolve an overcrowded room. It's easy for some to determine if a room has too much in it; however, what is too much for one person may be just right for another. You may be one who likes lots of decorative items; if this is the case, it may be more difficult for you to determine if your room has too much. Here's a tip we use with our clients that will help you gain a sense as to whether you have gone overboard with your decorations:

1. Choose one area of a room that you like to enhance with your favorite knickknacks, such as a shelving unit in your family room or the fireplace mantel and hearth area.
2. Remove all decorative items from this area (not the TV, stereo, etc.).
3. Stand back and take in the simplicity that has resulted. Surprisingly, many of our clients share that they can breathe better just looking at the empty space.
4. Being realistic, we don't expect you to leave this area void of decorations, but we do want you to think about what you put back on display. Slowly return the items with a plan in mind. Pay attention to the bagua station within which this area falls and choose items to correspond with that station.
5. Make sure you leave open space in this area. Metaphorically, open areas represent opportunities. In feng shui, open space is not considered empty but rather an area that holds potential.

If the eye is constantly moving from one conversation piece to another or if the room looks like a museum with a multitude of items on display, then the movement through, and the flow of the room, has been compromised.

The simplest way to remedy overcrowding, of course, is getting rid of items. It can be helpful to establish a schedule for thinning out items like toys, books, CDs, and other media. If you have too many pieces of furniture, pull one or two pieces.

Aside from reducing and removing items, there are other solutions. Following is a chart describing common problems we often see that need correction in order to bring balance and health to a room. We have included simple, no-cost remedies for each situation in the following table.

SOLVING OVERCROWDING

PROBLEM	SOLUTION
Too many patterns	Cover one or more of the patterned items with solid fabric
Too many magazines	Use a basket to hold magazines you want to keep
Too many books	Display the ones that are important or can be used in a bagua sector
Too many items on shelf	Reduce by being selective; group like items together; allow for open space
Too many collectibles	Store half of your collection; rotate pieces
Too many items not used	Keep what's appropriate for activities of the room

Overcrowded rooms irritate and agitate, inhibit open communication, and create a feeling of disharmony. These rooms are examples of either extreme yin—an excess of small items in a space; or extreme yang—an excess of large pieces of furniture. Both are stagnant and impede flow and movement in the room, which directly influences both individual behavior and group interaction. Remember TCM's definition of health? Crowded rooms do not allow for unobstructed flow; therefore cures are needed.

By now, after doing the exercises in this chapter, you should easily be reading your space, developing your ability to adjust and correct what is wrong, and finding appropriate and meaningful enhancements for your home. All of this will help you connect positively with your physical environment.

Chapter 9

Clearing Clutter—Keeping It Simple Is Not As Simple As It Seems

"De-junking isn't just getting rid of some unnecessary objects—it is getting control of your life."

—Don Aslett

CLEARING CLUTTER IS a love-hate endeavor; you really want to get rid of your unnecessary stuff but hate the idea of doing it. Most of the clients we work with are committed to the project but completely overwhelmed. We often hear such comments as:

Where do I start?
I've tried before but never get very far.
What if I pitch something that I will need after I throw it away?
It's hard to get rid of a gift; what if I hurt someone's feelings?

If you feel overwhelmed, defeated, indecisive, or guilty because of your messes, take comfort in knowing that you are not alone. Although your piles and "hidden treasures" are personal, clutter is a common problem shared by people of every age, gender, and socioeconomic background. That's right—we're all in this together.

Of course, there are those special people who were born with a sense of order and actually enjoy tearing into a closet or rearranging their shelves. You know who they are; there might be one in your family. We are convinced that there is a mutant gene that neat freaks have; it seems to skip every other generation, because they are a rare breed. If you are a clutter bug, it might be downright unnerving to be around someone who arranges her or his socks in a partitioned drawer according to color or considers organizing episodes a fun time.

What Is Clutter?

So how do you conquer clutter? Before we proceed, let's examine the topic. Following are some interesting observations about accumulation of stuff in contemporary times.

Your Clutter Is Not Your Grandparent's Clutter

What do you have that your grandparents did not have when they were your age? Well, for starters . . . computers, cell phones, fax machines, DVDs, VCRs, CD players, TV surround sound systems, video games, electronic garage door openers, more than one car, microwaves, digital cameras, camcorders, plug-in room deodorizers, a deluge of exercise equipment, and the list goes on. To sum it up, we have more stuff than at any other time in history.

Shopping Has Never Been Easier

Grandma either walked down the block to buy whatever was needed, carrying only the few bags she could handle, or if she lived away from downtown, her shopping had to be planned in advance or scheduled for a certain day because of restricted shopping hours, not to mention limited transportation.

For many of us, we jump into a car at any time of day and

often into the night, and in a few minutes we're at a mall, mega-shopping plaza, or superstore. We can order by phone through a catalog or use the Internet to receive merchandise within days. We pay by credit and debit cards, and we finance major purchases and obtain home equity loans in order to buy what we want *now*. We convince ourselves that items that are actually conveniences are necessities and rationalize that material goods will make us happier and improve our lives. Caesar's mantra "I came, I saw, I conquered" can be updated to "I saw, I wanted, I bought."

Teens Add to Clutter Problems

Teen power equates to money in the pocket, and their pockets have holes. The last three decades of the twentieth century gave birth to a powerful new purchasing group—teenagers. They, in turn, have become one big buying juggernaut. Here are a few facts that will throw you for a loop. If you have a teen in your home, this will help you understand how clutter accumulates right in front of your eyes:

- According to the August 2000 issue of *Credit Union Magazine,* teens spend more than $100 billion a year on clothing, food, and entertainment.
- Jupiter Communications reports that teens will soon outnumber adults shopping online. Teens and kids spent approximately $1.3 billion shopping on the Internet in 2002.

Clutter Is More Than an Accumulation of Material Goods

Physical clutter includes piles of paper, mail, clothes that don't fit, worn-out shoes, empty boxes, magazines, broken tools, gifts never used, and so on. Mental and psychological clutter includes projects that are started but never completed, intentions or goals never achieved, worries about finances, career plans that never get off the ground.

Disorder creates more mental clutter: guilt, frustration, depression, and other negative feelings. And your busy schedule has you overworked, overbooked, overcommitted, and overextended. Clutter will haunt, scold, restrict, and hamper you from living a meaningful, productive, and fulfilling life.

The Impact of Clutter

Physical and mental clutter go hand in hand; there is always a connection between a person's physical clutter and a person's emotional well-being, or lack thereof. Physical and mental clutter impacts your ability to concentrate, stay focused, be productive, begin or finish projects, or follow through with your plans or activities. Do any of these quotes from our clients sound like you?

> *I want to invite my colleagues to dinner, but I feel embarrassed because of the condition of our home. We have boxes that have sat unpacked since we moved into our home three years ago. To tell you the truth, I don't know where to begin.*

> *I finally realized that the mountains of papers, stuffed files, and the accumulation of magazines and catalogs that litter my office act as physical barriers that prevent me from starting a catering business and achieving my personal goals.*

> *My feeling out of control is directly related to my clutter being out of control. No wonder I don't get anything accomplished.*

> *I opened an envelope that had sat on my desk for over three months. It contained a check for $1,895.00 that came as a result of my request to*

liquidate a savings account. It was buried beneath piles of paper. I felt
stupid and angry because I knew my inability to handle my clutter
reflected my inability to handle my finances.

Clutter impacts your life in a number of ways. You can't find
what you need when you need it. It can make you feel overwhelmed, causing arguments between family members, alter your
social life, make you less productive, and promote procrastination.
More important, clutter takes up space you need for items and
symbols that support, motivate, and inspire you. To live with
clutter means that you choose disorder over order, turmoil over
peace of mind, and chaos over clarity. By hanging on to items that
no longer serve you, you give preference to what is obsolete, outdated, worn out, broken, not liked, not used, or not valued.

Your environment mirrors who you are, influences your
behavior and actions, and promotes or hinders positive change.
What does clutter say about you? How does it influence your
behavior? Does it allow for positive change to occur? Or does it
keep you stuck in the past, unable to achieve your goals or even
visualize what it is you want out of life? Clarity and awareness are
precursors to taking action; if you feel confused and lack a sense of
direction, it is difficult to make positive change in your life.

Most of our clients discover the deeper meaning and implica-
tions of their clutter *while* they are clearing their stuff. There's no
need to solve the mystery of why you collect and accumulate clutter;
you don't need to enter into counseling to get at the root of your out-
of-control situation. Whatever lessons you are meant to learn will be
revealed to you. Remember the quote from the movie *Field of Dreams*?
"If you build it, they will come." The same applies with your decluttering endeavor: Clear it and the lessons you need to learn will come.

This is a new approach—sort out your life by sorting out
your junk. Remove the barriers to a happier, more fulfilling and

rewarding life. Because your physical environment houses much of your clutter, feng shui is a logical approach to dealing with and understanding your clutter plight. Feng shui teaches that what blocks, hinders, or prevents easy movement and circulation in our bodies, mind, and physical spaces will ultimately make us ill emotionally, physically, and spiritually. Congestion, disorder, chaos, and confusion are not signs of a healthy space.

Before you can implement any feng shui cures, you must clear your clutter. What sense does it make to move your furniture to foster communication, use colors that soothe, or use a symbol that instills confidence if your clutter shuts you down, makes you tense, and mirrors your inner turmoil? Nothing takes away from an atmosphere of well-being, balance, and harmony more than clutter.

✳ Client Story: Released from the Past

Sherry, a workshop attendee, raised her hand and surprised us when she blurted out, "You changed my life." She had attended a previous workshop of ours conducted at a conference for singles. "It was the part about clutter in the basement; you said it could mean that someone was living in the past, not able to move on in life," Sherry said. At the time Sherry attended this workshop she had been a widow for over ten years and her husband's belongings were still in her basement. Her mother and aunt had both passed away the year before. Furniture from their estates was also stored in her basement. "I felt obligated to keep everything," Sherry admitted.

Sherry said that our remarks about the relationship between clutter in the basement and living in the past nagged her for days. Finally, she called a friend and asked her to come over and help her clear out her basement. As her friend toured the basement, she noticed the labels denoting each of Sherry's deceased relatives on the boxes. Sherry's friend exclaimed, "My goodness, your basement is full of dead people!" Although the statement was abrupt, it opened her eyes. After shedding a few tears, they both devoted the weekend to thinning out the basement. Sherry selected meaningful items from each of her loved ones and made donations of the remaining articles. "I immediately felt free, as if a heavy burden had been removed. This is what I needed to move on in my life." After that weekend, Sherry's life began to change.

The story had a Cinderella ending. Six months later Sherry met a wonderful man and is now married to him. Before then she was never able to keep an intimate relationship intact.

Eliminate Negative Overload

It is crucial to weed out negative influences and replace them with positive enhancers. Not only do you need to consider the usual piles and stacks of clothes, papers, magazines, toys, unwanted gifts, or a plethora of inherited items, but you also need to evaluate what we call "environmental clutter."

Conflicting colors, a multitude of patterns, irritating noise, hallways lined with boxes, or bulky furniture aggravates clutter problems. Just one or two of these issues can throw you into a feng shui frenzy. Take, for example, the home office of one of our clients. It was littered with papers, stacks of books, and boxes full of useless junk. The walls were covered with plaid wallpaper containing yellow, turquoise, and white, and a framed mirror hung over the computer. It was no shock to us that no one wanted to work in this room.

Location, Location, Location

To the trained feng shui "eye," your clutter speaks volumes about you. What clutter consists of may vary from person to person; however, the location of clutter usually indicates certain problems that we all share. Following is a chart that pinpoints the problem that is associated with the location.

LOCATION OF CLUTTER	COULD INDICATE
Entrance of a home or office/ business	A lack of concern about first impressions or fear of relationships
Inside a closet	An inability to deal with unfinished business or painful issues
In a kitchen	Caretaking responsibilities that are overwhelming; resentment
Beside your bed	Inability to make effective change in your life; desire to get away
On a desk	Overextension; frustration; fear of letting go or need for control
In a corner behind a door	Stifled feeling, detachment from others
Under a piece of furniture	Concern with appearances
In a basement with old collections or inherited items	Living in the past; difficulty moving on in life
In a garage	Procrastination; put off dealing with issues or allow what is urgent to become a crisis
All over	In denial; overwhelmed and angry

Workshop attendees invariably share their surprise at the accuracy of these insights. One woman pointed at the kitchen on the chart and blurted out, "This is too creepy—is someone peeking in my window? My kitchen is a continual mess, much like I am, because I have to take care of my family and an elderly mother. I love them, but I am overwhelmed."

Getting Started on Clutter

Eliminating a mountain of clutter can seem like climbing Mt. Everest—that is, if you don't have a decluttering plan. The benefits of such a plan are twofold: first, it will help you concentrate on the how, where, and when; and second, it will optimize your efforts by creating conditions conducive to clearing your messes. Before proceeding with your strategy, it is important to learn the Five Cardinal Rules of Decluttering.

1. Clearing clutter is different from organizing. Decluttering has to do with assessing and deciding what to keep or eliminate. Organizing has to do with creating a system and bringing order to what you have. Organizing is a part of decluttering, but it's not a substitute. You can clean and organize clutter; we've seen it. Boxes of seasonal decorations not touched in ten years, neatly taped and labeled; precisely stacked piles of papers; a closet rack full of outdated, outgrown clothes arranged by color; or a shelf full of obsolete technical manuals in chronological order, all unopened for over twenty years. All are examples of organized clutter, but organized clutter creates some of the same problems as disorganized clutter. First, get rid of your clutter, and *then* organize.

2. It gets worse before it gets better. You have to tear out, rummage, sort through, rip up, and throw away. You must read, try on, evaluate, experience guilt trips, deal with indecision as to whether to keep or ditch an item, and still remain sane. This is messy work, so just know to expect the storm before the calm.

3. Set realistic goals. If you want to set yourself up for failure, try telling yourself that you can clean all of your closets in a day. Try one closet, one shelf, or one drawer at a time; you are more likely to finish what you start. Your small victories will help motivate you.

4. Be easy on yourself. "Progress, not perfection," is a powerful bit of wisdom from AA's Twelve Step Program. If you can't complete your task in the time allotted, maybe you need to be more realistic about the time needed to complete your project.

5. More time and space may not be the solution. You can probably solve your clutter problem with the time and space you have. Instead of more time, better time management seems most effective in dealing with being too busy. That includes paring away some activities that take you away from more important tasks or goals. Sometimes more space can be helpful, but adding more space can also be an invitation to add more stuff.

All right clutter bugs, now that you've had your lecture, let's get started by deciding where, how, and when to start your clutter-busting venture.

Where Do You Begin?

Choose three trouble spots in your home. A trouble spot could be a pantry, basement, or home office. From those three, ask yourself which area would benefit you the most if it were decluttered and organized. If you are torn between two choices, choose the room or area that would be easier to tackle.

When Do You Start?

First, determine what time of the day you are most productive. Are you raring to go in the morning, afternoon, or evening? Of course, if you have children, you may have to set time aside for decluttering after they go to bed. If you work outside your home, make sure you prioritize this task and schedule it into your day. Next, choose two or three days of the week and mark the days and times on your calendar. Set a timer for one or two hours and work for no more than the allotted time. As eager as you are to rid yourself of your mess, it is not necessary to do it in one day; the important thing is to stick to your schedule.

How Do You Get Started?

Most people make the mistake of tearing into their designated room or area without setting a goal and establishing a plan of action. For the sake of helping you create this plan, let's assume that you are going to tackle your home or business office. For some of you, clearing your office of clutter may be a day out of your busy schedule; for others, it might take anywhere from one to three months to complete the task at hand.

1. Write down five decluttering tasks that you want to accomplish for the week within the office space. This can be as simple as listing five single-sentence statements. Research has shown that goals are more likely achieved if put in writing. Make sure you choose five simple duties such as going through a box of receipts, thinning out your Rolodex, or emptying the trash can. The idea is to set yourself up for success, not failure.

Remember, there is no rush; if your office is anything like we think it is, it didn't get to that state of chaos overnight. So what if it takes you three months to clear out your clutter and reorganize your office. Remember the Cardinal Rules of Decluttering by setting realistic goals.

2. If you are overwhelmed, think you will not follow through, or lack discipline, find someone who will hold you accountable. It could be a friend, family member, colleague, or feng shui professional. Whoever you ask, tell her or him that you need their help, not their reprimands or lectures. A feng shui professional will help you plot your course of action and set regular telephone meetings to help you through this process. Whoever you choose, share what you accomplished for the week and what you want to accomplish for the upcoming week. Our clients admit that this is one of the most effective tools for completing their clutter-clearing goals.

3. **Choose a starting point in the room and determine your work pattern.** You can go around the room clockwise, counterclockwise or from upper to lower levels. Whichever pattern you choose, stick with it.

4. **Start small by clearing out a set of shelves or a file drawer.** Use a timer and work for one or two hours; no need to have a marathon clutter-clearing session.

5. **As you are clearing your area, make a list of items that might help you organize this cleared-out area.** What is amazing is that those with real clutter problems usually have an assortment of plastic bins and containers that they have been saving for a rainy day. Don't run out to buy anything, as you probably have all the organizing aids at your fingertips. Get creative; if you need a box to hold your canceled checks, a shoebox is an ideal container. If you want something a little more decorative, cover the box with newspaper, construction paper, or leftover wrapping paper. Hold on to cardboard boxes that come your way or visit your local grocery store if you need boxes in other sizes. Make sure you label the contents of your boxes along with other pertinent information such as the month or year.

6. **The first time you go through your stuff, throw out anything you know is trash.** Now, get rid of anything that is broken or cracked and that you have no plans of repairing. After that, you have to evaluate whether something is useful or meaningful to you or not. If you can't decide, put those items in a container with a lid and mark it "Undecided—3 months." Move it out of the office and put in a temporary holding station such as a basement; go through it again in three months. Most likely you will not be able to recall the contents of this container. At this time, decide whether any items can return to your office, be used in another room, or be sold or given away.

7. **Once your system has been developed, stick to it.** If you get overwhelmed, take a break or start up the next day or the following week.

8. After clearing your litter from one designated area, organize the space. You do not have to wait until the entire office is cleared before organization takes place. If you have eliminated the mess on a shelving unit, go ahead and organize the items you have chosen to keep on those shelves. By doing this, you immediately benefit from your decluttering efforts. You've just gone from dysfunctional to functional.

Feng Shui Props

Let's face it; cleaning and clearing out your stuff may not be your idea of a fun time. To enhance your clutter-clearing activity, you need to implant mood enhancers into your environment that will keep you motivated, focused, and at ease. You'll be surprised at the end result these small features will bring about.

Aromatherapy

According to John Steele, leading aromatherapy expert and advisor to several well-known fragrance companies, the introduction of aroma into a space can alter a person's mood within ten seconds. How can this be? Because our sense of smell is controlled by the limbic system, a part of the brain that produces a totally emotional response; logic plays no part in our response to aroma. Although of few of you may not respond in like fashion, most will find that certain aromas can bring about positive shifts in mood:

- *For an uplifting boost*—bergamot, cedar wood, jasmine, lemon, or lime
- *For motivation*—any citrus, peppermint, or juniper
- *To relieve depression*—clary sage, geranium, jasmine, lemon, lime, ylang-ylang, or peppermint

- *To relieve mental strain*—basil, gingerroot, peppermint, or rosemary
- *To ease nervous tension*—lavender, neroli, orange, rose, tangerine, or ylang-ylang

Don't have essential oils, candles, or diffusers? Let your kitchen come to the rescue. Add any one or two of the following from your refrigerator or your spice rack to a simmering pot of water in order to create your own aromatic delight.

- Lemon, orange, or lime peel
- Cinnamon sticks, ginger, or whole cloves
- Peppermint extract
- Any fresh herbs such as thyme, rosemary, or basil

A word of advice: Twenty or thirty minutes of exposure to aroma is all you need.

Music

According to Don Campbell, author of *The Mozart Effect,* music is a powerful influence on behavior, mood, learning, and even physical health. It has been found that listening to Mozart, for example, can improve concentration, while Gregorian Chants can reduce stress. Depending on your situation or mood, listening to music as you clear your clutter may be more than just "music to the ear." Here are some influences from different types of music that might prove helpful:

- **For a sense of order needed for study or work**—slow Baroque music such as Bach or Handel provides a stimulating environment for study or work

- **For improved memory and concentration**—music by Haydn and Mozart
- **To promote active movement**—fun and peppy rock music by such artists as Elvis Presley or Elton John
- **To bring about relaxed alertness**—ambient or New Age music without a strong rhythm such as Steven Halpern
- **For improved performance and strategic thinking**—Beethoven and Mascagni

How much time is needed to experience the effects? As with aroma, all you need is about thirty minutes to reap the benefits.

Lighting

If the idea of ridding yourself of your litter and mess depresses you, how would poor, dim lighting impact you? Here are some lighting tips:

- If you can, let the sunlight fill the room by opening drapes or raising shades. This will invigorate you *and* reveal the layers of dust collecting for so long.
- No windows in the room or working in a basement? Use the highest-wattage bulb your lighting fixture can handle. If possible use full-spectrum light bulbs or at least bulbs that emit white light instead of the yellow cast of incandescent lighting. You will see the area better and the brighter light will be uplifting.

Know that feng shui cures cannot work their magic when clutter blocks the way. Understand that serious ongoing cluttering can be a sign of emotional distress. Take charge today and experience what happens when you let go of your clutter.

Section III
Feng Shui Room by Room

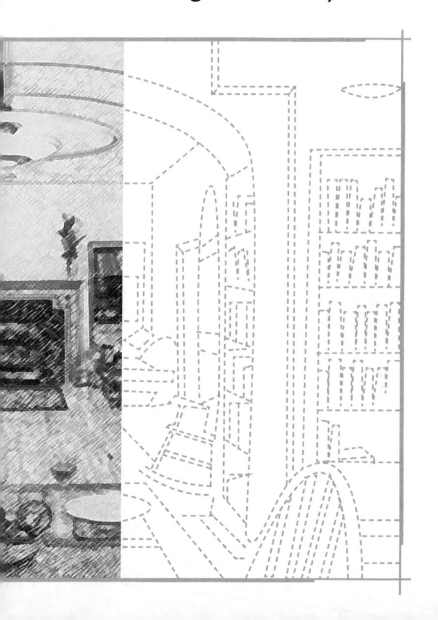

Chapter 10

The Room Evaluators

"Whatever your decorating style, feng shui principles will help you design a home you want to live in."

—Sharon Stasney

ROOM EVALUATORS ARE the key to assessing any room in your living space. Now that you've learned how to weed out negative features throughout your living space, you are going to learn how to assess each room in your house or apartment so that you can create or introduce positive features. Often you intuitively know when something is wrong with your living space—it just doesn't feel right. The Room Evaluators will help you to translate your intuition about what is wrong into concrete information on which you can act.

Take notes as you explore these questions in each room. It may be helpful to ask a friend to help you and provide an objective view.

What Is the Function of the Room?

Before you address any room, you must first consider how much time is spent and what activities take place there. How do you and your family use this room? This might seem obvious at first, but depending on your lifestyle and personal needs, you may be using a room for something other than its intended use. For example, if a dining room is being used as a place to handle household finances instead of as a dining area, then consider making it into an office. Or if your family needs a place to congregate and interact but the family room is sitting empty, then adjustments need to be made.

Here are some questions to ponder that will help you assess the functionality of your rooms or space:

- Are you stuck in traditional thinking that forces you to keep the typical rooms found in a house or apartment? For example, do you really need two rooms for dining, or do you really need a guest room? In feng shui, any room that sits idle or becomes a catch-all area is considered stagnant. Flow or movement is therefore, impeded.
- What is missing in your dwelling that you would like to have? For example, do you need a space for sewing, a hobby, or library?
- Are you willing to change that spare bedroom to a room that will allow you to have what is missing in your dwelling and that would better serve you or your family?
- How flexible are you? Maybe that guest room can be adapted to be both a guest room and a home office.

This is important, so give it some thought.

Should This Room Be More Yin or Yang?

Some rooms are meant for quiet activities (yin), while other rooms are meant for action (yang). In feng shui, yin and yang are opposites meant to complement, balance, and complete each other. For you to feel healthy and balanced you need appropriate amounts of time devoted to both work (yang) and rest (yin); if you take one to an extreme, you're out of sorts. The same applies to your living environment. Living in any extreme situation is not good for your mental, physical, or emotional health.

To refresh your memory about yin/yang, see the following chart.

YIN/YANG FEATURES

Yin	Yang
Quiet	With sound
Small	Large
Curving	Straight
Reading	Talking
Sleeping	Awake
Meditating	Exercising
Soft colors	Strong, vibrant colors
Dim lighting	Bright lighting
Watching TV	Playing Ping-Pong

Some rooms will be predominantly yin, while others will be predominantly yang. Those rooms that are considered yin are the bedroom, the bathroom, or a library. Rooms that should be predominantly yang are the kitchen, family room, or a playroom. The dining room is like a chameleon: it should be more of a yang room but needs to turn yin when the occasion arises. For example, while the dining room may be where large family holiday dinners take place, it's also the room for a romantic candlelight dinner.

Here are some general yin/yang guidelines:

- Even though a room might be predominantly yin, you still need to bring in some yang features. Conversely, a room that is predominantly yang also needs some yin features.

- You can infuse a room with yin by closing the drapes, using dim lighting, or by adding softness, such as using a table-cloth on a table. You can bring yang into a room by opening the drapes, using overhead lights, or allowing hard surfaces to remain by keeping the tablecloth off the table.
- Look to the activity to help you decide how you will use certain areas within your living space. For example, if you want to meditate or do yoga, seek out a yin space. If you want to do aerobic exercise, seek out a yang space.
- Don't go against the yin or yang nature of a room. In other words, a bedroom (yin) is a room of rest and relaxation, so refrain from using bold, bright colors on a large scale in this room. A splash of red is one thing; all four walls painted red is called "over the top."

Does the Room Look and Feel Balanced?

Ask the magic questions. Does the room look and feel top-heavy? If this is the case, you might see shelves running all along the top part of the room, crowded with a surplus of decorative items, along with an ornate chandelier hanging from the ceiling. Heavy beams may stretch across the ceiling or a ceiling fan with dark-colored blades may become the focal point because the room has light-colored walls and is sparsely furnished. Either would be an example of a top-heavy room.

Does the room feel and look bottom-heavy? If this is the case, you might see heavy furniture with accessories, plants, and lamps that sit low in the room. Prints, paintings, or other art objects sitting on the floor and carpeting or rugs so loud in design and color that other items in the room receive little attention can make a room feel bottom-heavy.

Does the room have too many furnishings and decorative

items on one side of the room? Is the furniture placed or positioned so that it looks balanced? Sometimes this is hard to spot
and not as obvious as you might think. To determine this, draw an
imaginary line down the middle of the room. Now, check to see
what is on each side of the room. If the room looks as if it is in a
ship sitting lopsided on the ocean, then the weight in the room is
out of balance.

Does the Room Look Welcoming?

As you enter an area or room, pay attention to what greets you.
Does it look and feel welcoming? Does it beckon you to enter? Is
the focal point intriguing or does it tell you to stay away? Anything
that treats the senses is a sure winner in making a room look and
feel inviting. It's like setting up a seduction scene; as a person
enters your dwelling, he or she is caressed by what they see, hear,
touch, smell, and taste. Comfort features such as an area rug inside
your entrance, loose pillows on a couch, comfy slippers by a fireplace, a lovely painting of rolling mountains, the pleasant smell of
coffee brewing or bread baking, a candy dish filled with chocolate
truffles, the sound of water coming from a fountain, and lush
plants make any room or area an inviting and alluring place to be.

Think about what makes a room uninviting. Overcrowding
and clutter, of course, counter your welcoming efforts, but what
about extreme rooms? For example, a room that is too tidy or
orderly sends a message that nothing can be touched or moved; a
room that is too sparsely decorated feels austere and stern; and a
room that is overly ornate lends to a feeling of formality and pre-
tense. None of these situations are welcoming.

Are All Five Elements Present?

You need a predominant element and a second, less-predominant element, along with splashes of the other three elements. Make sure all the elements—Fire, Earth, Metal, Water, and Wood—are present in the room. For example, if you see that you have no Water represented in the room, a simple glass bowl filled with water and sprinkled with flower petals or leaves is a quick and attractive addition. Refer back to Chapter 3 to help you with your evaluation. In evaluating the elements, keep in mind that certain elements work better in some rooms than others. For example, because the kitchen is a very yang (active) room, it best not to use Water as the predominant element. Water is the most yin (quiet) of all the elements, so it would go against the yang nature of the kitchen.

As you apply Room Evaluators to your living space, we hope you begin to fully understand the intimate relationship that you have with your living space. Whether you live in an old family house, just rented your first apartment, or move frequently because your spouse is in the military, bonding with home, however short or long the stay, is as important as bonding with a loved one. As you move through the next chapters, we hope you will come to have a new appreciation for the spaces in your dwelling and how they can best serve you.

Chapter 11

Transitional Spaces—
The Mood-Setting Themes

"When we walk through our front door, we should be able to leave the stresses and strains of the outside world behind."

—Jane Alexander

What Are Transitional Spaces and Why Do They Matter?

Have you ever entered a building expecting to go straight to your destination and instead discover a dark entry hall as you step inside? You find no sign or directory that gives you a hint of what floor or hall connects you with the office or apartment you hoped to visit. An uneasy feeling creeps up on you as confusion about what to do or where to go next sets in. Imagine guests visiting your home and feeling the same way as they cross your threshold. A visitor's first impression of your home should be pleasant, not depressing. Likewise, your entry should embrace and celebrate you rather than repel you. Think of a loyal pet waiting eagerly for your arrival home.

Houses and apartments vary in sizes. Some have a threshold that opens right into the main gathering place; others have a small entry area; and some have a long foyer. Whatever you have, there is a feng shui strategy for each that creates a graceful entry, enhances a threshold, or energizes a passageway as you or your guests navigate spaces in your home.

Importance of Transitional Spaces

Transitional spaces are important because they are the flow-through spaces inside and outside of your home such as entries, thresholds, hallways, staircases, and pathways. Transitional spaces play several important roles. Besides acting as pathways moving people from one place to another, they are:

1. Your introduction of you to arriving guests
2. The link between the busy pace of the world outside to the slower pace of the world inside
3. A place to pause and set your mood for crossing the next threshold

Thresholds—"Open Sesame"

What are thresholds? Not many people give thought to them. We encounter them as we enter our homes and we cross them as we enter each room. As in our homes, we also cross thresholds in our lives. Crossing thresholds can be the beginning of an adventure, marking the critical moment when your mood changes as the implied purpose of space becomes clear. Metaphorically, the thresholds you cross in your home can represent life-changing events in your life. The threshold underlines the transition you make from one place to another.

The symbolic act of stepping over a threshold so many times throughout our day sends powerful messages we rarely notice consciously. If that threshold does not embrace us positively each time we cross it, over time our positive mental psyche wears away. We become less aware of opportunities that connect us with intimate relationships or fail to notice a new career option, or miss an opportunity to enhance our health and mental well-being. "How can this be so?" you ask. The following client story illustrates the connection between crossing thresholds in our homes and in our lives.

Client Story: Stumbling Through Life Is Second Nature to John

John was always disorganized, often showing up for work late and frazzled. His wife, Teresa, bought him a feng shui consultation for his birthday in the hopes of changing this pattern. When we arrived at the home, three young children and a room full of toys greeted us. We toured the one-floor ranch style house, asking John questions about his daily routine and especially about the time before he leaves for work in the mornings.

We noticed that the door he used to exit and enter the home had an uneven lip on the threshold. He mentioned often tripping over it himself. Next as we walked through the door, the protruding splinters and nail heads in the door-frame snagged us both. He apologized and mentioned the two suit jackets he recently had mended as a result of the same thing happening to him. When he took us outside, we discovered another hazard. Having three young children in the home, many toys and bicycles littered the pathway to the car.

Just the act of leaving in the morning seemed to leave John in a frenzy. The daily path to his car required him to carefully avoid being tripped by obstacles in his pathway or being snagged by protrusions in the doorway. Leaving for work in the mornings was definitely a stressful time for John. He told us that by the time he arrived at the office, he was so frustrated that it took him until noon to get focused.

After assessing the situation, we recommended John find a way to manage the children's toys that were always cluttering the driveway and repair the doorway. Two months after our visit, Teresa called to update us on the home situation. While repairing the threshold and door frame, John discovered he enjoyed bringing it back to its original splendor. Feeling a sense of accomplishment, John built a toy box for the kids (a place for the scattered toys), and a bicycle rack for their bikes. He was getting to work on time these days and the kids were seeing more of him. Hmmm, we wonder why that happened? Could it be that because we showed him a way to eliminate the hazards he encountered along the physical pathways in his home, that his struggles to get to work on time and lack of focus at work disappeared? Our recommendations for John guided him in changing his physical surroundings which, in turn, led him to a less stressful way of navigating life.

In our lives, crossing a threshold is an occasion to transcend from one world to another. In John's case, having a hand in repairing the threshold in his home also repaired other areas of his life. He now spends more time with the kids, feels better about himself, and is no longer frazzled. Teresa is happy, too.

Eliminating the Negative

No matter where you live, whether you own or rent a home, check for the negative messages in the thresholds of your living space, as detailed in the following chart.

PHYSICAL FEATURE	NEGATIVE MESSAGE
Cracked cement or broken steps on landing	Having problems with keeping relationships together
Door hard to open and close	Career opportunities hampered; mindset is stuck or stubborn, not seeing what is there
Paint peeling off door little by little	Detaching oneself from others little by little
Dead or damaged vegetation	Lacking energy or in poor health
Pathway to outside landing or inside hallway is obstructed or covered	No direction in life; indecisive
Clutter all around threshold	Fear of moving forward and, therefore, putting up barriers
Dust bunnies in corners, base-boards, and hanging from ceilings	Many areas of life are left unattended

Tips for Accentuating Exterior Thresholds and Entrances

As humans we need to see clearly identifiable physical reminders that take us from one state of mind to another. Without these cues for transition we would not be prepared to experience the next sensorial episode of a space. The sequence of approaching, passing through, entering, and using a building does more than affect our experience of it; it changes our inner state. We become more receptive to what our surroundings are saying to us, which triggers a transformative process in our innermost being. Our transitional spaces offer inviting glimpses of pleasures to come. A moon gate is a perfect example of a threshold that invites us to experience the mystery beyond.

Make the main entrance to your home clearly distinguishable from all other entrances. Especially if you live in an apartment, distinguishing your special part of the block is important. Follow these suggestions:

1. Place a brighter bulb in an outside lighting fixture, making the threshold more visible at night. This works like a lighthouse.
   A lighthouse never gets lost. It lights the way for opportunities and people to come into your life.

2. If allowed by your condo or apartment association, place colorful plants or topiaries on each side of your entry or landing to define your threshold.
   Let the world know you have a defined purpose in life.

3. Hang a decorative flag or mobile outside your door.
   When the breeze blows, it will wave to passersby, attracting smiles of positive energy to your door.

4. Look for, correct, or camouflage anything broken or in disrepair. Place potted plants in poorly landscaped front or back areas where you enter. If allowed by your landlord, paint flowers or other outdoor scenes using the cracks in the concrete or porch surfaces as stems for flowers.
   Each time you walk out your door a garden of abundance will greet you, making you smile and sending you on your way.

5. The word *Welcome* or a feature that implies the same within the first few seconds upon approaching the threshold should be visible.
   This tells all that you are approachable and welcome friendship, and it gives a hint that the entrance is there.

6. Pathways to your threshold should be free from all obstructions and wide enough for a person to navigate

without feeling cramped. Check for overgrown vegetation, broken concrete, holes, and so on. If you own your home, prune the vegetation. If you are a renter or lessee, ask maintenance to prune the plants, or get permission to do it yourself.

Navigating a difficult pathway may also metaphorically reflect struggles on pathways in life.

7. If you use a side door, garage, or porch as your main entry, all of the previous in this list apply. Porches, laundry rooms, garages, back doors, and so on should be clear of clutter and junk. A porch especially should offer refuge and be given the same consideration as an indoor room.

   Honor your status as the Master or Mistress of your home. Make sure the entry you regularly use reflects this. Framing a garage entry door with your favorite calendar pictures personalizes that entry. Hanging twine on hooks on the laundry room wall and hanging doll clothes or using clothes pins to hang favorite calendar pictures brings a little whimsy to the space.

Defining Indoor Transitional Spaces

The space into which your door opens is the suspended dimension between the activity of arriving and the shift of mood involved in settling in. This space should sustain the mood set by the threshold. No matter the size of your entryway, your living space should unfold one step at a time until you or your visitors reach the main gathering space. It should possess an unobstructed flow of energy that will meander throughout all the rooms in the home. There should be no second-guessing as to which way to go.

A person who crosses
this threshold sees
no clearly defined
boundaries, leading to
a state of confusion.

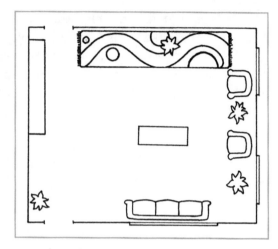

The adjustments made to
the room create clearly
defined boundaries,
allowing a person to
move with ease
throughout the space.

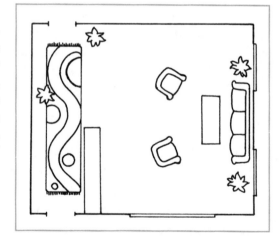

Clarity and legibility simplify any journey. A roadmap and a
highway use mile markers and exits to let drivers know where they
are. Nature uses the riverbanks of the moving waters, mountain
ranges and prairies to define its boundaries. Humans use body language, words, voice inflections, and facial expressions to give

clarity to a message. All these cues help us find our way whether we are traveling or interacting with others in conversation.

Likewise, cues in an entryway or hallway help us define and interpret the space. These transitional spaces should invite a procession along the private and semiprivate rooms of a home and have clearly marked messages wherever there is a need for a direction change or mood. For instance, a closed door may symbolize "don't enter without knocking." The gentle flowing of chiffon fabric at an open French door leading to a terrace or balcony may beckon one to come hither. The change of floor texture from carpeting to ceramic tile may send a message that this room is more utilitarian in function.

If your entrance is extra long, treat your senses to a meandering, poetic journey to the center of your dwelling by infusing scent on one side, then sound further down on the opposite side, then visual stimulation back across the foyer. Continue the stimulation of the senses until you reach the threshold of the next space within your dwelling. Try some of these ideas:

SIGHT
- Use plants to create the peaceful feeling of nature.
- Turn on an overhead light in the entry to spotlight the threshold.
- Use ambient lighting in lamps that lead the eye from one area to another.

SOUND
- Place a water fountain near the threshold to create the peaceful sounds of nature.
- Play music on the stereo that draws guests down the entry and into the next space.
- Place a chiming clock in the entry area so guests arriving on the hour and half hour can be announced by the chiming clock.

SMELL

- Place an accent table with lamp and bowl of potpourri in the entry space.
- Use plug-in scent holders to infuse the entry with a welcoming scent.
- Set out a bowl of fresh fruit.

TEXTURE

- Place a bench or chair with decorative pillows or throw in the entry area.
- Cover tile or wood floors with a plush area rug.
- Place a basketful of soft, clean footies near the threshold for guests to wear at informal gatherings.

TASTE

- Set out a dish of chocolates or mints.
- Set out finger appetizers on a small table at the end of the foyer.
- Place a tray with glasses of wine or champagne near the end of the entryway.

Making the Most of Transitional Spaces

If you have a folding screen, use it to define a threshold or separation of a space. You could also create a makeshift screen by placing plant hooks in the ceiling along the width you would like to create for a threshold. Hang or swag a curtain, sheet, or other fabric to either side of the hooks to indicate an entrance. Fishing line comes in handy to run through the hooks and is strong enough to hold many fabrics. Also, don't rule out dental floss; it is almost as versatile for home décor and repair as duct tape and probably almost always around. Hanging ribbons, beads, or other lightweight elements can also create a definitive boundary.

If living room and dining areas exist in the same space, area rugs or a painted floor cloth can be used to define the two spaces. Changing the texture on the floor creates another threshold. Also, strategically placing plants will create a boundary for separation and an opening/threshold or entry can be defined by the heights of the plants.

If you need some complexity because all the walls and trim in your dwelling are one color, hang a symbol over door frames—for example, a eucalyptus leaf hung over a bathroom door symbolizing purification, or a bouquet of roses with ribbons hung over a bedroom door symbolizing romance. Accentuating the purpose of each space in our homes at thresholds and entryways provides the clarity we need when navigating our physical environment, and thus, as we navigate our pathways in life, we are able to clearly define thresholds of opportunity for abundance, relationships, and well-being.

Inside, use a high-wattage bulb at the door to spotlight the arrival of a visitor and to focus attention on you for safety purposes. If your entry opens directly into the main gathering space, place a small area rug inside the door and a plant to help define an entry, which will aid in the mood change and transition to the main area of the room.

Place a scarf or decorative fabric over a portable dinner tray table or other small table close to the door of entry to provide a place for keys, gloves, and mail. The ritual of setting these items down allows you to change your thoughts from go-go-go to relaxation.

Hallways

Most hallways lie within the interior of a dwelling. Feng shui treats them as pathways. Visitors may use them, but, in contrast to the entryways or foyers, they are semiprivate spaces and you may choose to feng shui them in a more personal way. Hallways should support and nurture your goals and aspirations, because you travel through them daily as you go to work or other events in your life and again when you return home. Inner hallways, those positioned away from the entry, can reflect a more personal theme than an entry hallway. In many large corporate offices and government buildings, along hallways you may see pictures of leaders who have come before or certificates and awards honoring the important people of a company or organization. As the current CEO or leader of the company walks down these halls, a feeling of exhilaration may appear as if he or she is being cheered along the way.

The same can be said of how you treat the hallways in your home. For instance, if you seek approval and attention from loved ones as you grow in your career path, you might hang pictures of loved ones on the hall wall along with other symbols that support your dreams. We recommended this cure for a young male client who had low self-esteem. When he awoke each morning, he needed to have a path of honor to walk where everyone was cheering him. On the wall he added picture frames containing his affirmations to remind him of and keep him focused on his intentions and goals. Our client responded to the cures so well that later in the year we found ourselves invited to his wedding.

Don't place pictures in your environment out of obligation, such as those of people with whom you have an estranged relationship or, in your mind, of people who serve no purpose on your road to success.

To someone who has reached the pinnacle of success and wants to slow down, we recommend creating a garden path using pictures of nature, or focus the pathway around leisure activities by hanging pictures of fishing streams or golf greens. The theme of your goals and intentions determines the boundaries of the pathway. Make sure you use lighting appropriate for the journey you wish to make. Brighter lights move you faster and draw attention. More subdued lighting, such as over each picture, can imply stops along the way.

Stairways

Feng shui takes the position that the way we travel to and from our spaces can mirror the way we travel through our lives. Stairways hold a prominent place in those journeys. For that reason, they should always be clear of clutter to prevent accidents. Railings should be strong and trustworthy. Pictures, lighting, and other items that direct the eye should be less complex than in other areas so the eye sends a steady, rhythmic message to the feet.

Unless we are elderly or have a health problem, we rarely pay attention to how stairways affect us. They can twist and turn and have landings halfway. Stairways elevate us to a higher level not only in a structure but symbolically in life as well. Familiar phrases such as "Climbing the corporate ladder," "Reaching another rung on the ladder," or "Each step is a benchmark in our journey to success" are symbolic sayings that reflect climbing or going up. Stairways also allow us to descend to lower levels. "Getting our head out of the clouds" and "Coming back down to earth" come to mind as metaphoric analogies.

Some stairways are so steep that going up or down them requires us to tackle them cautiously. Still other stairs are built so they create a rhythm in our stride, allowing us to navigate up or down with little effort. And many people, including both of us, use stairs as a convenient temporary shelving to place books, stacks of papers, shoes, and clothing to be carried up or down the next time we navigate the stairs.

We know of a wonderful place located in Hocking Hills, Ohio, called Cedar Falls. Visitors have one of two choices to get to the falls. One is to follow a meandering trail down through the forest and then back over a wooden bridge, where Cedar Falls can be viewed from the bottom. The second choice is a stairway, designed by Japanese architect Kio Hizume, that leads from the picnic area to the bottom of the falls and can be navigated with little effort. It is specially constructed so that people of all shapes and sizes can climb or descend the stairs easily and not get tired. Each riser acts like a landing, providing a place for visitors to pause and giving them a new point of view from which to appreciate the beauty of the falls. Hizume, in his design, varied the distance between each step so that the climber not only alternates legs in the descent or ascent, but establishes an internal, almost subconscious rhythm.

The stair risers are long from front to back, so you have to bring your second foot to the same level with your first before stepping to the next riser. When climbing or descending the stairs, one gets a sense of rhythm that is almost like walking a labyrinth, but instead of going left and then right as labyrinths are designed, one goes up or down with a pause in between.

The stairs at Cedar Falls in Ohio are a wonderful example of taking an architectural feature that we normally connect with getting us from one floor to the next and using it to make music. These stairs did this by creating a rhythm in our pace and adding tone using the sound of our steps. As we ascended and descended the stairs, it was as if a melody was created underfoot. After experiencing those rhythmic stairs at Cedar Falls, we always try to replicate that same rhythm in some form within our clients' spaces.

Spiral Stairways

Spiral stairways have different connotations in different places and cultures. Spiral staircases in European castles were almost always located in towers used for incarcerations. Most of us are familiar with the Jack and the Beanstalk story where Jack climbs what seems like a never-ending spiral vine and afterward encounters the giant. Traditional Chinese feng shui practitioners refer to spiral staircases as corkscrews that can skewer the heart of a home and thus the heart of the owner. These examples imply that spiral staircases could lead to doom.

In American theater, spiral staircases onstage act as props, adding an architectural feature to the show. Lofts in urban cities sometimes have spiral staircases leading to an upper level to conserve space. Some fire escapes have alternating turns at each floor level, which forces those who descend them to follow the same pattern as one would when descending a spiral stairway. The message implied is that we must pay attention to and show caution when traveling these types of stairs. Because of these special characteristics, spiral staircases require special attention:

- Directions on spiral stairways must have good legibility and clarity.
- Spiral stairways must be well lit both from above and below.
- No objects that create obstructions to navigation should ever be placed on the risers.
- Spiral staircases can seem like they are floating, because of the open risers; placing plants (silk or real) under the risers can help in negating the feeling of insecurity when climbing or descending them.

A spiral stairway can prove to be an asset, providing an interesting design feature if you follow these simple guidelines.

✳ Client Story: Toe-Tripping Stairs

One of our clients, Abby, a young woman whose main complaint was that her family was always falling on the stairs, had unknowingly created her own problem. In examining the space, we noticed photos of all shapes and sizes hung in an arrangement that followed the zigzag pattern of the stair risers as one would travel up or down. To add to the problem, the picture frames were of different sizes and held pictures of celebrities and European vacation trips, inviting the family to examine them more closely; thus, the complexity of the wall took their minds off of traversing the stairs safely. We even found ourselves having trouble climbing the stairs, as we wanted to look at the pictures. In addition, the carpet runner covering the stairs was red with a triangle pattern. Talk about a double whammy! The feet wanted to run but the eyes wanted to meander. No wonder they were falling on the stairs.

These are the recommendations we made:

1. Move these interesting pictures to another place in the home where they can be appreciated—safely.
2. Place on the wall along the stairs still-life pictures, making sure to hang only a few along a horizontal plane.
3. Place a small, round rug at the bottom of the steps, as a circular shape physically forces the eye to focus and will negate the motion created from the triangles on the red runner.

Falls up and down the stairs ended as the urge to travel up and down quickly disappeared. The attention of family members traveling the stairs stayed focused on the task. Doubtless many broken bones were averted by these simple changes.

More Stair Tips

- Place a basket or other container over to the side of the stairs, both at the bottom and top to place items in them that you want to transport up or down. Take care to place the containers where you cannot trip over them.

- Keep wall hangings along stair walls simple; the more complex a display, the more danger of tripping going up or down.
- If you stare at a blank wall as you are descending the stairs, hang an inspirational quote in that space to greet you each time you descend. Research has shown that an idea presented a minimum of six times eventually becomes an automatic action in a person's life. Don't hang anything that would send a negative message in this area!

Tips for Creating Welcoming Transitional Spaces

1. Include a seat or bench in an entryway. If there is a choice between left or right, always choose the right side. The majority of the world's population is right-handed, so turning right when entering a space is only natural.
2. Set the mood for you or a visitor by letting your home unfold one step at a time. Tickle the senses by subtly guiding movements of your guests with an aroma, sounds, a change in floor texture, lighting, or stimulating view. Let the pathways unfold gently, keeping visitors intrigued.
3. Place in entryways and hallways only items and symbols that send positive messages to you and others.
4. Keep hallways and other transitional areas free of clutter. This allows energy to move freely and unobstructed throughout a dwelling.
5. Hang moving objects to attract attention in a particular direction. For example:
   - **Wind chimes**—when the door opens the breeze from

outside makes it chime. This sound announces your guest or welcomes you home.

- **A mobile**—you can make a mobile by hanging wooden, glass, or plastic beads, bells, or spoons on a narrow ribbon or other light string such as dental floss or fishing line.

6. Keep personal things such as bills, receipts, etc., out of site in a covered basket or box.

7. Place a small book containing daily devotional quotes or a framed affirmation about your purpose in life on a welcoming stand reminding you daily of your life intentions and goals.

✳ Client Story: Crossing the Threshold

When we first met Greg, he was concerned about a promotion at work. In fact, he talked of little else during the visit. During the tour of his home we noticed a poorly defined path that led to the front door entrance. Although there were other adjustments, we decided to concentrate on exterior recommendations.

With enthusiasm and a lot of pent up worry, he started the landscaping project. Over the span of four weekends he cleaned up the outside landing to his home, added new landscaping, painted his front door, and fulfilled a longtime request from his wife of changing the doorbell. It now sang beautiful songs of birds when the doorbell was pushed. Putting in new landscaping gave Greg a challenge that he proudly conquered, and he gladly accepted the new responsibilities for upkeep of the area. Seeing the change of the entryway to his home gave Greg a fresh new outlook, which in turn affected his attitude at work.

A few weeks later, he was called into the supervisor's office. Greg shared with us that he walked down the long passageway between the cubicles and stepped over the threshold of the supervisor's office. He said that although he crossed that threshold to the supervisor's office many times, this time, as he entered, the act took on new meaning. In sharing his story, he recalled that it seemed as if a new chapter in his life was about to begin.

To his relief, Greg received a promotion and raise, starting immediately. Crossing that threshold presented him with new challenges and responsibilities just like the new landscaping. The raise in his pay was music to his ears just like the new doorbell. As Greg turned and crossed back over the threshold of the supervisor's office, he said he felt a new vitality and actually bounced a little as he walked back to his office.

Had the threshold to Greg's home and landscaping been left unkempt, Greg's energy at work could possibly have reflected the same and he might not have gotten the promotion. If so, then crossing that threshold would have a different meaning. As he turned to walk out of the office, he might have been crossing the threshold to an unknown future.

Chapter 12

The Gathering Room

> "Living rooms speak volumes about your personality and how you view the world, so make it an accurate account."
>
> —Terah Kathryn Collins

WHETHER YOU CALL IT a family room, a living room, or the great room, the gathering room is where you, your guests, and family members converge to talk, entertain, watch television, or play games. It's also usually a place where you can curl up and read a book, watch *Casablanca* for the fifth time, or sink into the couch as you gaze upon a roaring fire in the hearth. Given all the different activities that take place, such a space might be better named the multipurpose room.

Feng shui can do more to improve your social life or family relations when applied to the family/living room than any other room in the home. It can change a bachelor's space from an isolated sitting room to a frequented gathering place or make a "for show only" living room into a space where guests do not want to leave.

✳ Client Story: Directing Traffic

Kevin and Estelle loved their new house and were eager to make it the home they had always wanted. When we met with them, they explained that they wanted visitors to tour their home starting in the living room, then the dining room, followed by the kitchen, with a final destination of the family room, where the entertaining would take place

We were relieved to see that the living room sat to the right of the foyer. Research has shown that most people bear right when entering a space due to the fact that over 90 percent of the population is right-handed. Still, as people entered their home, they turned right, then turned back around and headed straight to the kitchen. It was apparent that guests were confused as to which way to go.

After careful inspection we discovered the following culprits:

1. The living room appeared cold and sterile because of a hard tile floor and very little texture.
2. Tension existed due to an imbalance of the elements. The predominant elements were Fire and Metal, with the Earth element completely missing. This imbalance was seen in the red and white pattern of the wall covering (Fire), a red leather sofa and chair set (Fire), and white, high-gloss tile floor (Metal). Because Fire melts Metal, they oppose each other.
3. Furniture placement actually blocked the entrance, making it difficult to enter the room.
4. The room looked and felt lopsided because most of the furniture was on one side of the room and sat at an angle with respect to the walls. Given the makeup of the room, the angled furniture arrangement only added tension to the room.

Before—the entrance
was blocked and too
much furniture on one
side of the room made it
appear off balance.

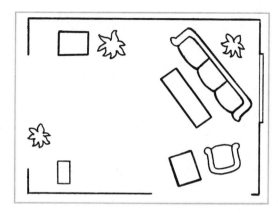

After—easy access to
the room and proper
positioning of the
furniture made the
room more inviting.

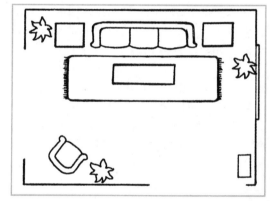

In order to remedy the situation, we went on a scavenger hunt around their house and made the following changes:

1. The red leather furniture in the living room was just what the mundane family room needed, while the tan, textured sofa and chair combo that sat in the family room was the ideal match for a cold, hard-looking living room. Besides adding texture to the room, the furniture introduced the Earth element by way of the tan color. Of all

the elements, Earth lends to a feeling of stability, comfort, and homeyness.

2. An area rug that sat in front of the family room fireplace lessened the sterile quality and Metal presence represented by the glossy white tile. The family room was carpeted, so the area rug wasn't missed.

3. We rearranged the furniture so that the sofa became the focal point of the room. End tables were placed at both ends of the sofa, creating a symmetrical and balanced ensemble. This arrangement also eliminated the angled layout of the room.

4. We moved the chair that prevented people from easily entering the living room, allowing for easy access and maneuverability.

The original problem was solved; guests immediately turned to the right and entered the living room. In fact, Kevin and Estelle had a new, "good" problem to deal with: their visitors never wanted to leave the living room! Oh well, that's another story.

What Is a Gathering Room?

The first step is to determine which room is the gathering room in your home. If you only have one room to sit in, it's not hard to determine. But be aware that a living room may not be your gathering room if little time is spent there or if it is actually a showroom for guests to observe as they head to other parts of your home. This is not uncommon in a house or apartment that has both a living room and a family room or den.

If you find that you are not using a room as it was intended to be used, consider another use for the room. Maybe that unused living room should become a much needed study or library.

Now apply the Room Evaluators (see Chapter 10) to your gathering room.

What Is the Function of the Living/Family Room?

The gathering room is typically a high-use room, especially if it contains the television and/or other electronic equipment. A gathering room should foster good communication, encourage interactive activities, and promote a positive ambiance. The family or group should come first in this room, and then the individual.

Should This Room Be More Yin or Yang?

A living/family room used by your family or guests should have more of a yang influence; however, having a yin area will contribute to maximum functioning. This could be a reading corner with seating for one or a desk with a lamp on it that is positioned away from the main seating arrangement. This table should help you determine how to bring yin and yang aspects to the room.

YIN FEATURES	YANG FEATURES
Solitary seating for quiet reading, looking at photo albums, or taking a cat-nap	Group seating arrangement inviting conversation or watching a game on TV
Tray sitting on coffee table or ottoman with two wine glasses and bottle of wine, plate of cheese, crackers, and grapes	Cushions on the floor surrounding a large ottoman or coffee table with a board game and a bowl of popcorn
Closed drapes or blinds inviting curling up on the couch with a good novel and chenille blanket	Open drapes or blinds allowing streaming sunrays to energize the room
Soft, easy-listening music	Loud, bouncy music

Does the Room Look and Feel Balanced?

Balance is a very important aspect of feng shui. Ask yourself the following questions about the room you're evaluating.

Does the Room Feel Top-Heavy?

This happens when there are many items along the top part of a room and heaviness seems to loom overhead. Floor-to-ceiling bookshelves filled with books, mementos, and other knickknacks can have this effect. A shelf that runs along the perimeter of the ceiling with an array of decorative items, ceiling fans, ceiling beams, and lights positioned along the beams can create a top-heavy feeling. If the room is top-heavy, the eye goes up. The first line of action is to remove some of the items near the top of the room or rearrange items on high shelving to balance the weight. A silk plant with vines that fall down over the edge on the top shelf will lighten that shelf and redirect attention downward. Try these other tips:

- Where you have lots of items, remove every other one to lighten the load on the shelf.
- Place fabric, napkins, or any like item under some of the items and let fabric drape over the edge of the shelf.
- Position lighting to shine down rather than up.
- If you own your condo or home and have leftover paint that is the same color as the ceiling, paint the beams the same color as the ceiling. The same goes for the fan blades on a ceiling fan.
- Remove a few items from the shelf and hang them on the wall.

Is the Room Bottom-Heavy?

Look around the room to see if you have an overabundance of items that sit on the floor. Or you might have dark-colored furniture and dark flooring, which takes the eye directly to the floor. In either situation, the room will feel heavy and weighted down. If you have too much on the floor, simply remove some of the items. Here are some other tips:

- If you notice an abundance of dark colors found near the floor, replace some of them with light-colored items.
- Use or arrange plants with leaves growing in an upward direction on coffee tables, end tables, or a desk.
- Apply a stencil around the perimeter of the ceiling to draw attention up.

Is There Too Much Furniture on One Side of the Room?

As simple as this may sound, it's amazing how often we see this. If one side of the room looks weighted, it makes you feel lop-sided and off balance. Of course, the obvious solution is to rearrange the furniture. This is not as difficult as it sounds once you become aware of the situation.

A quick tip would be to imagine your room divided into four quadrants and identify what furniture is in each area. If you find one or two quadrants with either too much or too little, consider eliminating, adding, or rearranging items to bring the room into balance.

When judging the room for balance, don't be concerned if you have placed items on the floor, in the middle area, or toward the top of the room. What we are referring to is an apparent overload that appears out of sync with the rest of the room.

Does the Room Look and Feel Welcoming?

Do visitors tend to gravitate toward your gathering room—or do they head for your kitchen? Does your family go to the gathering room for most of its communal activities—or do they retreat to their rooms? An inviting gathering room can be vital to your family.

What Greets You As You Enter the Room?

In a gathering room, your eyes should immediately locate the focal point; think of it as the anchor of the room. A focal point brings gravity to a room, helping people feel centered and grounded. Just as gravity keeps us attached to our planet, so does the gravity of a room keep us secure in our surroundings.

A room will always have a focal point, albeit sometimes not always the one you want. Ideally it would be a fireplace, a centrally located coffee table, an oriental rug, or a large painting on the largest wall in the room. On the other hand, a focal point may be a gun collection, a stack of boxes, or a torn and frayed area rug. Determine what the focal point is and correct it if necessary. Next, see if the room is filled with an overabundance of items or has too much furniture. If it does, it will feel overcrowded. Nothing should compete with the focal point; rather, all other aspects should help create a balanced room.

If you are lucky enough to have a fireplace in your home, just know that it demands center stage. The fireplace, in all it various forms, has always been an integral part of human existence and humans are genetically encoded to respond to it. Whether it is the campfire of a primitive tribe, the hearth used to prepare food and provide heat for early pioneers, or the gas-burning fireplace in your condo, whatever holds and contains fire for the benefit of humans is considered the physical *heart* of the dwelling. It is not coincidental that the floor before a fireplace is called the hearth. If you drop the last *h* from *hearth*, you have *heart*!

If your family room's focal point is the hearth, arranging your furniture around it will provide physical and emotional warmth. If your focal point is a large painting, be sure it sends the message you want. Paintings of pleasant nature scenes are always appropriate as are scenes of people interacting or children playing. Be careful of a focal point that sends the wrong signal. One client had a large painting of herself over the couch in the living room and other photos as herself throughout the house. We tactfully told her that using herself as a focal point gave the appearance of self-absorption.

Following are other items that can be used as a focal point and the message each might send.

FOCAL POINT	MESSAGE IMPLIED
Seating arrangement in the middle of the room	Inviting for people to sit and talk
Large colorful area rug	Feeling of being grounded
Bay windows with a view of nature	Focus on nature; relaxing
Entertainment center with TV, DVD, stereo, etc.	Takes attention off interaction with others and instead focuses on being entertained

What Are the Comfort Features in the Room?

Comfort features are all about the senses. The senses are powerful vehicles that feng shui uses as conduits to human response. This is an underpinning of Pyramid feng shui.

Here's an easy way to go about this sensorial review. First check for anything negative such as unpleasant odors, cracked windows, loud or irritating noises, or a lack of items with texture. After you scope the room for harmful sensorial features, think about ways to activate the senses.

How Important Is Smell?

Just imagine the odor of garbage greeting your guests and you will know that it is downhill from that moment on. If you do nothing else, open the windows and air out the room. A word of caution: Be careful when using aroma; response to smell is all about emotion. It can also be very personal. You may like the fragrance of rose, but some may find it repulsive. Using a scent constantly can desensitize one from its effects. So use scents to evoke emotions when appropriate and only for a short period of time as its effects disappear after a half hour. Wondering about what scents to use? Research shows that most people respond positively to the aroma of food. Citruses, such as lemon and orange, are fresh and uplifting, while cinnamon and apple evoke a feeling of warmth and comfort.

Refrain from over saturating the room. If you've ever been around someone who used too much perfume, you know what we mean.

How Important Is Touch?

Think of all the ways touch can benefit you. It is therapeutic and comforting—a gentle massage, healing touch therapy, a hug, or cuddling up with a blanket. Nothing lends to comfort more than the sense of touch.

Of course, touch connects us to texture and tactility. Even the appearance of texture can conjure up the experience of touch. So, whether you see those soft, cotton throw pillows or touch them, you still experience in your mind the sensation of touch.

Imagine there is a very contemporary sofa in your family room—crisp sleek lines and smooth satin fabric. Now suppose you place a soft waffle-textured chenille throw on that couch. Wow! What a change. The message of the sofa went from "stay off me" to "sit down and get comfortable." Fabric is not the only way to bring touch into the family room. Carpeting, a crocheted rug, a woven place mat under a lamp, the brick of the fireplace, the smooth stone sculpture, and the grainy, knotty pine paneling all lend to an interesting array of touch experiences.

How Important Is Sound?

Imagine your dream family room with your favorite colors, furniture, and aromas. Now add the element of loud radio static. Common sense tells us that no matter how beautiful and pleasing an environment is, the element of sound can destroy or enhance the desired effect.

Think of all the noises you hear while sitting in your living/family room. At any given moment, you may hear the television blaring, people talking, the dishwasher running, the dog barking, the furnace humming, and the phone ringing. More than any other room, perhaps with the exception of the kitchen, the gathering room is a hotbed of sound. Give some thought to what you, your guests, or family hear while in this room. How inviting are these sounds? Sometimes you need the roar of laughter, the chatter of conversation, and the rhythmic beat of dance music while other times you need the stillness just to sit and gather your thoughts.

Most of all, expose yourself and others to the sounds of nature if possible. Some of you are fortunate in that you are able to open a window and listen to a gentle breeze and birds singing, while others can play music containing nature sounds or turn on the nature sound machine that your sister gave you on your birthday.

How Important Is What You See?

The most complex of all of the senses is sight. It enables you to absorb, filter, and interpret an immense amount of information when compared to the other senses—it is your principal way of gathering information. Unlike smell, sight demands that you think and use logic. What people see as they enter your family room is very important. Next to the entrance or foyer, this room is used to evaluate what kind of person or family lives in this house or apartment. Do they see views of nature, family photos, favorite mementos, comfortable furniture, and pleasing art? Or do they see dirty dishes, stacks of newspapers, and four pairs of shoes? Nothing takes away from comfort as much as clutter. Choose your symbols carefully; they influence not only you but other people who visit your home as well.

Light is also an important consideration. It's advantageous to have both overhead and task lighting for specific activities that are done in the room (for example, a reading lamp). Turn up the lights to induce activity (yang); turn down the lights in order to relax (yin). When considering light, you also need to realize the biological influence that it imparts. Hormones that affect your mood are released by light, as seen in its extreme form with seasonal affective disorder (SAD). Although most people don't suffer from severe SAD, many people are affected by the short days of winter. That is why it is a good idea that you use full-spectrum light bulbs in one or two of your lamps; it comes closest of all artificial lighting to duplicating the color spectrum of sunlight. Need a boost? Turn on that lamp.

Are All Five Elements Present?

Refer to Chapter 3, "The Five Elements," to help you assess what elements are in your room. A word of caution—it's best to stay away from using Metal or Water as the main element of a gathering room. Water is too yin and may put people to sleep, while a Metal room will appear rigid and formal.

You want your gathering room to feel comfortable and inviting, so how you combine the elements can make or break the desired ambiance. Using Wood as the predominant element will invite spontaneity, a sense of adventure, and lively conversation. Earth is probably the safest to use as a predominant element when it comes to creating a sense of comfort, but don't go overboard; too much Earth will look boring and actually make those in the room feel like they are dragging. Even though a comfy atmosphere is important, the family room still needs a spark here and there to invite activity and conversation; if you have too much Earth in this room, bring in some Metal features and use Wood accents for that extra punch.

Using Fire as the predominant element will definitely create a high-energy room. There's nothing wrong with this as long as you remember to use a strong dose of Earth features with a dash of Water here and there. Wood and Metal should also be used.

The following table details what that room might look like.

Focal point	Large print (picnic scene) over couch with wood frame
Walls	Deep cranberry red
Ceiling	White
Carpet	Tan
Sofa	Light beige leather (leather is Fire and beige is Earth)
Love seat	Same as sofa with tan, red, and ivory plaid throw
Side chair	Tan, red, and black tweed
Side tables	Wood
Coffee table	Wood with glass-top insert
Area rug under coffee table	Cranberry red with tan, black, and white border
Drapes	Ivory with black and red piping
Accents	Plants, silk flower arrangement, lamps, and various art and decorative items

✳ Client Story: Me, Myself, and I

Cassie asked us to evaluate her great room. "This is my favorite room but my family never uses it," she told us. After doing an assessment of the room and making a few recommendations, we finally detected the problem: the placement and positioning of the furniture. Even though she had a sofa, love seat, recliner, rocking chair, shelving, and a wood dinette set, none of it was arranged so that the family could sit together at one spot within the room. Without knowing it, Cassie had made the room function primarily for her by creating several comfortable venues for all of *her* activities: yoga, exercising, reading, and doing paperwork.

To solve the problem, we positioned most of the seating around the fireplace, placed the TV on a rolling cart so that it could be moved as needed, placed the dinette set close to the kitchen, and created a small private reading area for her. When it was time for her to do yoga or exercise, all she had to do was move the coffee table that sat on top of a large area rug.

To her amazement, her family joined Cassie in the great room that evening. They ate dinner, played Monopoly, and watched some TV. Now the room truly functioned for the family.

More Tips for the Gathering Room

1. If you want the gathering room to be supportive and nurturing to children or anyone who is experiencing stress, use the Earth element as the predominant element. Beige, tan, terra cotta, and peach are good Earth colors, and ceramic objects or rock collections are good Earth items.
2. For a little punch, bring in Fire element features. Red flowers, some candles, art depicting people or animals,

and leather items are a few ways to introduce the Fire element into a room.

3. Ideally, the gathering room should have a public and a private area.

4. Seating for main occupants should have a solid wall behind it. If this is not possible, create the illusion of a wall by using a screen, desk, small narrow table, or tall plants.

5. The gathering room should have adequate storage, proper lighting, and pathways that are easy to maneuver.

6. If you have small children, have a separate area for their personal items.

7. The television should not be the focal point. If possible, keep the television in a cabinet with closing doors. If you do not have this, you can cover the television with a tasteful scarf or tablecloth when not in use.

8. If you have several pieces of electrical equipment in the gathering room, bring in live plants. Research has shown that they mitigate the effects of electromagnetic fields.

9. To induce open and comfortable conversation, position some seating at right angles.

10. If possible, use floor pillows, as this is an excellent way to make people feel grounded. Children especially take to sitting on the floor.

Chapter 13

The Kitchen and Eating Spaces

"It's fun to get together and have something good to eat at least once a day. That's what human life is all about—enjoying things."

—Julia Child

WHETHER YOU COOK or not, Americans have deemed the kitchen to be the heart of the home. No other room evokes such emotion connected to fond memories of pleasant aromas, sumptuous meals, family gatherings, and intimate conversations as much as the kitchen. To be sure, a kitchen is more than an eating or cooking area; by its nature, it probably is the most heavily trafficked and, in some cases, the most popular room in a home. It serves as an entertainment hub, message center, and a meeting place for family and friends. For the creative cook, it is a favorite room; for those less inclined to cook, the kitchen is considered a work area. No matter what your activities tend to be there, whether the kitchen is spacious or small in size, it should be a happy and cheerful room ready to nurture and support those who use it.

If you enjoy cooking, the kitchen should reflect the personalities of those who cook in it. If two cook in the kitchen, each person's individuality should be seen in some form. An extroverted personality may have lots of utensils close at hand in colorful containers around the stove or work counter. An artistically inclined personality might arrange the pots and pans to reflect an aesthetically pleasing arrangement. Then again, a gourmet cook will have a proper place for each utensil and ingredient, making it easy to find at a second's notice.

Feng shui professionals can easily read a person from the kitchen's appearance. For instance, if the kitchen is fitted with white cabinets, white walls, and chrome appliances, then we are dealing with an industrious, hard-working person who is serious about her or his cooking and not concerned about connecting emotionally with others. This is a working kitchen, not a place that is inviting or evokes comfy emotions. Whereas a kitchen exhibiting fresh fruit displays, flowers, and lots of colors may reflect an individual who loves to entertain and enjoys the company of others. A clean and tidy kitchen that is individualized to the owner says, "I care for my well-being." An untidy, cluttered kitchen could send a message that the inhabitant of this space may be overwhelmed with care-taking or is just unable to nurture others. Whether you are a person who does not like to cook, or just doesn't have the time to do so, or are a person who lives to be in the kitchen, feng shui addresses each to promote mindful nourishment of the body and soul.

The Function of the Kitchen and Eating Spaces

These are the spaces where we receive sustainable nourishments for our bodies. In some cases, that nourishment may only be coffee or tea, or juice and a bagel, and in others, a four-course meal or large holiday celebration. The kitchen is where both memories and meals are made, as all five senses are easily triggered into action in these spaces. We should consider these spaces as the most important places for our physical nourishment. Our ability to protect our immune systems, to absorb vital nutrients, to increase our energy, and to connect us with happy aromas is dependent upon the value and care we give these spaces.

In many homes, the kitchen and eating area are the main clutter traps, collecting work brought from the office, book bags from school children, shoes and boots, umbrellas and coats. In America this happens often because the kitchen most likely is the first room we step into as we enter our dwellings. It has long been said by Eastern traditional feng shui that if the kitchen is visible from the entry we may spend all our time eating or worrying about food. Remedies such as adding a feature that directs the line of vision away from the kitchen or blocking the view altogether by placing a screen in front of the kitchen entry are effective.

Should This Space Be More Yin or Yang?

The kitchen is our room for sustenance. It actually can be considered a creation room for big meals when entertaining, for mini-meals quickly consumed, and sometimes for meals that heal what ails us. Yang energy dominates this space because the Fire element is ignited. We cook, bake, broil, heat, and mix our foods in this space. After the prep time, we eat. And, unless we are entertaining festively, our consumption of food and drink should happen in a more yin atmosphere to facilitate proper digestion.

The equipment tends to be yang as these items imply activity and usually are the largest pieces of furniture in the space. The stove produces Fire, the sink produces Water, and dishwashing, whether by hand or with a machine, produces noise. There are lots of smooth reflective surfaces to facilitate ease of cleaning, and many areas with task lighting. All of these activities keep the kitchen energy yang.

The eating space can be either yin or yang depending on the type of meal being eaten. Preferably breakfast time should be more yin, allowing you time to focus on your day's schedule. Less excitement is better for digestion. So if you are a person who makes time for breakfast, place a yellow bouquet or candle in a metal container on the table to facilitate focus and clarity of mind. Metal is good for focus and the color yellow promotes clarity of mind.

During a lunch or dinner meal, for those of you who enjoy entertaining, bringing in colors of red-orange, bright yellows, and using pictures or displays of a variety of food can set a very yang and festive mood.

If you are less inclined to entertain but appreciate good nourishment, bring color in when you prepare meals and experience the yang through your food choices. Lots of fresh green, red, and yellow fruits and vegetables on display accomplishes the festive mood without the party. An all-white kitchen can be very yang but the sterile feeling projected also can decrease the appetite. For the finicky eater, use green plates; green makes food appear more appetizing.

A reason you might want to increase the yin in your kitchen and eating area is if you wish to lose weight. Besides the color white, the color blue tends to decrease the appetite. Blue also is known to reduce blood pressure. You may find you eat slower under its influence, giving time for the stomach to signal the brain when it is full. If you need that extra little nudge to help you lose weight, use a blue plate or blue place mat.

If children are at the table, focused attention on their needs is important and sometimes having fun at dinner or breakfast creates wonderful yang energy, which can produce cozy yin feelings in the tummy.

If the meal is to be a romantic dinner for two, then turning out the lights and lighting candles sets a yin mood that could be a precursor to yang activities later. What is important is balancing both yin and yang to support the activities occurring within the space.

Does the Room Look and Feel Balanced?

The kitchen naturally has heavy appliances to serve the purpose of the space. As a result, the balance of the space can be lopsided due to poor design. If you rent, you may not have the option of redoing your kitchen. Adding a brighter light bulb in task areas can help draw attention away from heavy appliances and balances the weight. Reducing the collection of small appliances on counter spaces also helps. Small kitchens can't stand much clutter, so contain it as much as possible. Larger kitchens, conversely, can handle more complexity by adding small appliances on counters, more vibrant colors, and larger pieces of furniture such as buffets, an extra table, and more chairs.

To draw attention from overhead weight that can't be removed, if possible focus all lighting on a table surface. Candles can be used for this purpose. Sometimes, if the eating space is small and the table can be pushed against one wall, a small lamp can draw attention away from overhead weight. And if you like displaying collections of baskets, pottery, or other collectibles above eye level for show, the less complexity you have on your table, the more balance you will have in your space. Many times we visit homes where wonderful collections are displayed all along shelves positioned close to the ceiling, while at the same time large centerpieces on tables or hanging chandeliers over tables compete for attention.

Does the Room Look and Feel Welcoming?

Does your kitchen, dining table, or counter space display piles of mail, bills, and other clutter all the time? Eating spaces are negatively affected when clutter permeates. Clutter implies "holding on to." Is this what you want to do with all the food you eat? Probably not. Clutter, as you have already learned in Chapter 9, affects our psyche and therefore our digestion. Why display financial obligations and junk mail that haunt you when you eat? They certainly won't aid your digestion!

If you have both an eat-in kitchen as well as a dining room, then most likely the dining room may be used less frequently than the kitchen eating space. If the dining room has only a part-time purpose, it loses its vitality during those long periods of nonuse. You might consider the dining room a multipurpose room, using it for other family activities, as a part-time office, or even as a prep space when counter space in the kitchen is not available. If you have the luxury of a large kitchen and other rooms in your home to cover all your needs, and you do not use the dining room much, consider changing table centerpieces regularly in keeping with the seasons and holidays. Wipe off dust weekly from the tabletop or change the tablecloth if you use one. To keep this room's vitality fresh, open windows regularly if you have them. Display fresh flower arrangements and add aromatherapy.

Are All Five Elements Present?

Chances are, all five elements are present in your kitchen. The kitchen is the easiest room in which to incorporate all five elements at once. The heating elements on the stove represent the Fire element. The sink produces the Water element. Utensils show off the Metal element. Dishes and clay serving containers, baking stones, and other earthenware show off the Earth element. Growing fresh herbs in the kitchen or displaying pictures of vegetables or cookbooks with herbs and vegetables on the cover incorporate the Wood element. Wood cabinets also represent the Wood element. The Fire element is the most dominant in the kitchen because it must be activated to cook our foods. Water is the next most dominant because it is usually used to mix ingredients and to cook with. Most foods contain some form of liquid, as juices flow from meat as well as vegetables. Obviously, cooking utensils and most containers for cooking are metal. Earthenware is usually used for baking. Using spices and herbs as ingredients once again brings in the Wood element.

Having all five elements in eating spaces is just as important as in the kitchen and can serve more diverse purposes. Determining which element dominates the space will depend on the atmosphere you seek at your dining table.

For instance, a romantic dinner for two might incorporate the dynamic duo: Fire (candlelight) and Water (wine). Together they make steam. If you seek an opportunity for good communication in a team atmosphere (such as discussing ideas for a family vacation), this goal can be facilitated by incorporating the Water element, represented by a pitcher of ice water with lemon (don't forget yellow for focus) and the Earth element, represented by square-shaped or beige place mats, or a ceramic bowl of fruit as the centerpiece.

What if you wanted to promote trust and security for a child who is less inclined to speak during family mealtime? Allowing the Earth element to dominate the space can promote a secure feeling. Eating on earthenware dishes, using square place mats, using a small terra-cotta flowerpot for a napkin holder, or positioning seating so as to imply a square shape can bring the Earth element to the table.

The element represented by the table shape will dominate the space; add the other elements so that all are represented. Flickering candles send the Fire element. Place mats in colors or designated shapes can bring in other elements.

Tips for the Kitchen and Eating Spaces

1. If when cooking you find yourself facing away from the kitchen entrance unable to see who is coming in, place a small mirror on the wall or place something shiny such as an aluminum pot on the stove to reflect motion behind you. That way your eye can keep up with the comings and goings within the space.

2. To invite vitality and draw people into conversation, place a circular object such as a round basket of flowers, a round place mat, or round-shaped pottery in the center of your table.

3. Soften glare in the kitchen caused by natural sunlight or task lighting by strategically placing earthen objects on the countertops. Earthenware can help absorb the light. Use bamboo place mats or add a tablecloth to a glass-top table.

4. In dark or very small kitchens, use brighter light bulbs in task areas. The brighter lights will make the space feel more spacious and chase away any dreariness, especially on overcast days or for those who live in parts of the country where long winter months sometimes also mean many days without bright sunshine.

5. Use candlelight for a more yin ambiance in the dining space.

6. Kitchens have numerous tools that need to be close at hand. Containerize as many as you can in decorative pitchers, cans, and such, to eliminate a cluttered feeling. Keep all clutter cleared.

7. If you are trying to lose weight, remove magnets, pictures, and other representation of foods you are trying to avoid from the walls, counters, and the door of your refrigerator.

8. Use high-backed chairs for more formal dining mood and low-backed chairs for a less formal mood.

9. Cleaning your refrigerator can be a pain but caring for your food is synonymous with caring for the nourishment of your soul. Try scheduling this chore once a month while at the same time scheduling time to purge old items off of your to-do list and refreshing your goals and intentions for the next month.

10. Arrange colorful fruits and vegetables inside the front of the refrigerator like a still-life picture. Doing this may entice you to eat healthier on a regular basis, which is sometimes not the case for those of us who eat on the run.

11. If cleaning your kitchen is a chore that you hate, then think about this: In traditional feng shui, cooking is synonymous with money. Think of the task as symbolizing an investment in your future fortunate blessings.

12. If any side of your dining table faces a picture window, close the drapes or block the window with a screen to eliminate distractions while you dine.

13. If the option is available, enter your home through an entry that does not present the kitchen first. Otherwise, deflect the view using a folding screen, plants, or other pleasing object.

14. If you have an eating space with an east-facing window, position young children who tend to go slow in the morning so that they can see the morning sunrise.

15. If you're not into housecleaning, seeing the kitchen first each time you enter your dwelling can determine your mood for the rest of your day. Should this be the case for you, keep the space decorated simply and clutter free;

otherwise it will only serve as a reminder of one more chore you need to perform.

16. To empower a child with low self-esteem, occasionally place her or him at the head of the table during meals. Giving them the power seat builds confidence and allows them to lead for once.

17. The place in which you prepare and eat your food tells a story about your vitality and how you feel about nourishing your body. Therefore, honor your mind-body-spirit by making the kitchen and eating spaces sacred to your nourishment. Your health and your life depend upon it!

Chapter 14

The To-Do Rooms—
Office/Work Areas

"Home is so fundamental
we tend to overlook the
degree to which it affects
our work, our well-being,
and our overall
effectiveness."

—Victoria Moran

THE LINE SEPARATING the conduction of business at home and participating in family activities is being threatened. The popular trend of cocooning in the '90s has rebounded and come back in this new millennium tenfold and technology has contributed greatly to this recurring trend. Having a virtual office allows one to enjoy the environment in the home while putting in hours for the boss. Wireless laptops and other electronic gadgets allow us to travel throughout our homes doing chores, taking care of little ones, cooking meals, and even lounging by the pool. Home was never meant to be a place for conducting business twenty-four hours a day.

The desire for having hobby and craft workshops in our living spaces also permeates our culture today. As a result, we may be lured away from spending quality time with our children or significant other to work on a project. Other times, a hobby becomes a fun family activity.

Taking these facts into consideration, this chapter will focus on tips to enhance workspaces rather than just a home office, as many of our readers' situations apply to workspaces rather than a full-service home office. If you do have the luxury of having a separate home office, applying the feng shui principles in this book to your space will enhance it greatly.

What Is the Function of the Workspace?

Activities and functions performed in this space usually require focus and clarity of mind with reduced distractions and interruptions, and an atmosphere that promotes problem solving and the free flow of ideas.

Here are some examples of activities often performed in workspaces:

- Watching stock quotes
- Conducting day trading
- Creating art or crafts projects
- Sewing
- Operating a home-based business
- Processing bills and correspondence
- Making business appointments
- Performing tasks related to a hobby

No matter what the purpose is, a workspace requires some sort of focused activity. Even if you don't have a separate room devoted to the work at hand, where you perform these activities should be a comfortable, efficient, and enjoyable place in which to be.

Should This Space Be More Yin or Yang?

The activity performed will determine the yin or yang of the space. The following table will help you assess your space.

YIN ACTIVITIES	YANG ACTIVITIES
Concentration	Telephone calls
Thinking; evaluating; processing	Running shop equipment, saws, sewing machine
Problem solving	Operating pottery wheel
Online research; computer work	Hammering copper sheet
Knitting	Developing and practicing a new dance routine for exercise class
Reviewing manuscripts; writing music	Playing musical instruments
Reviewing recipes; planning menus	Building furniture

Other considerations:

- Are you left-handed or right-handed? From where is the main light source coming? A task light should be on the opposite side of the dominant hand to prevent shadows from obscuring your task.
- Do you perform both right-brain and left-brain functions in your workspace? Left-brain activities require concentration and focus such as paying bills or the task of cutting out a dress pattern or connecting a wire sculpture. Right-brain activities require creative and artistic approaches in work such as designing the wire sculpture or customizing the dress pattern to be different than on the picture. Create a space that nurtures both sides of the brain.

Does the Space Look and Feel Balanced?

Make sure that your workflow follows a comfortable path that keeps you efficient. Doing this saves time and reduces stress on you while in the end producing a better-quality outcome. For example, don't put the printer on the other side of the room from the computer if you need to have access to the information quickly each time you print or if you frequently need to remedy paper jams.

Do you have room to move around and work? Are the tools of your trade easily accessible? Is the weight or density of your space mainly on the floor in stacks of files or boxes of supplies, or in a desk too heavy for the space and loaded with clutter? Tools that you use regularly should be easily accessible so you don't have to dig for them. For example:

- If you have a workspace in the garage where you also park your car, installing hooks in the ceiling or along the wall allows you space off of the floor to hang hammers, levels, and other tools.
- Old wastebaskets or large plastic buckets left over from supercontainers of dishwasher soap or other agents usually have handles and are wonderful for small hand-tool storage, tape measures, sewing supplies, and craft items, and because of their handle, can be hung up off of the floor.
- Leftover paint needed later for touchups, nails, screws and bolts, buttons, beads, and sewing needles store well in condiment or canning jars. Rig a wooden beam in the closet, garage, or basement and nail or screw the lids into the wooden beam, then fill the jars with your items, screwing the jars onto the lids nailed to the beam. This is a space saver. You can have fun with the jars by decorating them with fabric, decals, or stencils.

Does the Space Look and Feel Welcoming?

For those of you who have to compete for space when working at home, the room in which the space sits must be included in the overall evaluation. If it isn't, and say, for instance, the space where you plan to do year-end taxes is surrounded by dirty dishes or piles of homework from children, your goal of finishing the taxes may be sabotaged. Apply the organizing and decluttering tips you have learned so far from this book to the area where you conduct your work activities. The more open space you have for hobby activities, the more inviting your space will be. The more organized your tools and accessories are when conducting your work activities, the more productive you will be. So create smiles by getting rid of piles!

Does the Space Incorporate the Five Elements?

In a home workspace, balance the elements to your advantage. For example, add Metal for focus, Wood for new ideas, Water for introspective problem solving, and Fire for the promotion of action.

If motivation is the energy you seek, add Fire:

- Red pencil can
- Turn on spunky music
- Work near animal prints

If you need space for concentrating and evaluating, like when working on a budget or your taxes, bring in the Metal and Water elements—Metal for concentration and Water for evaluation:

- Tall glass of ice water
- Brass letter opener or gold pen
- Circular (Metal) coaster for the water glass

If you need to stay focused but relaxed to read a manuscript, combine Metal and Earth elements—Metal for focus and Earth for comfort and relaxation:

- Sit in a soft, cushy chair (Earth)
- Use a metal bookmark, paper clips, or pen (Metal)
- Clay flowerpot to hold desk accessories or small tools (Earth)

If you have only one day to come up with some "out-of-the-box" jingles for a new client's advertising account, bring in the Wood element and Water element—Wood for generation of new ideas and Water for communication of those ideas:

- Glass paperweight (Water)
- Small healthy plant next to your workspace (Wood)
- Rectangular shapes (Wood)

Tips for Home Workspaces

1. Containerize items you use regularly in your workspace by using portable carriers so they can be stored away out of sight when not needed and brought out easily when you are ready to use them.

- Hanging shoe bags cleverly organize everything from pens, pencils, paintbrushes, stationery envelopes, scissors, paper clips, rubber bands, postage stamps, and even those pesky monthly bills. These bags can be hung inside a closet door and even right over the clothes pole if you have room.
- Baskets with carrying handles (including those plastic laundry baskets) work great when you have a load of work you've brought home and don't want to leave it on the

couch or table. Just drop the load in the basket when you step inside the door. When you are ready to tackle it, just pick up the basket and take it to your workspace. This allows you some time to separate yourself from "work" and take time to adjust your mind for some "R and R" before you return to your business mindset.

- Processing mail can sometimes be overwhelming, especially when junk mail and numerous subscriptions come at the same time. Place a wastebasket or other trash container close to the door so when you enter you can immediately separate and throw away junk mail, eliminating the clutter that occurs when it is ignored and left lying around too long. For those who have garages, the perfect place for the waste can is just before you enter the house.

- Use a small rolling cart and place all your containers with work tools and/or equipment on the various shelves. Find a place in a closet or a secluded corner in your home where it can be stored out of the way. When you are ready to tackle a job, just pull it out and set up your workspace anywhere.

2. Choose a room or space for your activity that has the least amount of outside distractions for you and does not impinge on others living there. When space does not allow this luxury, you can try these suggestions:

- Using a large piece of corrugated cardboard or science fair display board, create a folding screen on the top of a desk that sits behind a couch or on top of a kitchen island to separate your work from family activities. This board can be decorated with fabric, painted, or collaged with magazine pictures. When work is completed, the board can be folded up and placed in a closet or slid under a bed or couch until it is needed again.

- Temporarily repositioning a chair or table in a more secluded space of a room to conduct detailed work activities is also an option. Be careful, however, about your back positioning. If this forces you to have your back to a doorway in an effort to remove distractions, protect your back by also moving a tall plant or other object behind you and adding a reflective object at your workspace to alert you when someone is behind you. If possible, place casters on items you plan to move regularly to make this task less tiresome.

3. Glare on your work surfaces, computer screen, and reflective objects around you can be troublesome and cause serious eye fatigue. To eliminate these problems try these remedies:

- Position an umbrella to shield bright light from coming through the window. Place the umbrella handle inside a jar, vase, or any appropriate container weighted down with rocks, sand, or marbles to prevent it from toppling over. When the sun comes in too strongly, just open the umbrella. You still have your light but not the glare. This idea works just as well to diffuse an overhead light that can't be moved. Repositioning plants to diffuse light also works quite well, while at the same time connecting you with nature.
- If you are working at a glass-top table, throw a tablecloth, sheet, or set place mats over the glass top while working there. Doing this hides the glare caused by the reflection of light on the glass.
- Eliminating highly contrasting colors such as black and white, black and yellow, and green and white from around your workspace can reduce eye fatigue as well. Getting rid of high-contrast colors, especially around computer workstations, prevents the pupil of the eye from contracting and

expanding constantly in an attempt to stay focused. You will find that you can work a lot longer and more efficiently by correcting a situation like this.

- Get rid of or cover any busy patterns such as plaids, triangular designs, etc., that also cause eye fatigue when concentrating on a project.

4. A big issue with not having a specific room for an office or workspace is not having tools and equipment readily at hand. Here are a few ideas to remedy the problem:

- For easy access and convenience to regularly used tools of your trade, a lazy Susan on your desk or work counter saves space while at the same time allowing you ready access to any tool you need. The lazy Susan can store more things that you need at arm's reach in less space than can be stored on top of your work surface without one. Just spin it around and reach for your pencil jar, paintbrushes, tape dispenser, or whatever.

5. A workspace or desk that is too small for the work activity being performed will cause frustration and stress; the person trying to work in the space may feel that his or her ambitions are restricted, making the completion of projects a problem. A large open workspace creates the impression of having the space to get things done and makes it possible to accomplish more. If your workspace is small, follow these tips to prevent frustration:

- Clear all unnecessary items from the workspace.
- Place only necessary items needed to perform tasks intended for the space. For instance, if your space is in the kitchen and you use the space to process and pay monthly bills, don't have dishes and miscellaneous kitchen tools sitting all around the workspace. Have pens and pencils close

by, a desk calendar, your checkbook, and a basket, box, or other container to hold monthly bills.

- The color yellow can help you focus on detailed tasks, while the color aqua can work to reduce stress when you are trying to concentrate. Paint your pencil can aqua or use a vase of that color and add a yellow flower to it.

6. Electronic equipment in your workspace generates electromagnetic fields (EMF). Studies show that the most harmful levels of EMF reach up to thirty inches in front of a computer or television and three feet to the rear. Plants need to be within these distances of equipment to provide protection, as they clean the air and filter the EMF.

Good choices of plants include:

- Spider plant
- Aloe vera
- Peace lily
- Boston fern or other type of fern

7. Ideally your workspace should have as much natural light as possible. Sunlight greatly stimulates the flow of vitality in a space, creating a dynamic and thriving atmosphere. If sunlight does not shine on your workspace, try one of the following suggestions:

- Use light-colored shades with incandescent light bulbs.
- Use low-voltage halogen lamps that emit a bright white light in a space.
- Add a small mirror to the space to help reflect light onto the work surface. The mirror can serve a twofold purpose by also letting you know who is behind you should your back be facing out.

8. Tall structures on either side of your workspace, such as a refrigerator or tall cabinet or bookcase, may give the feeling of

being overshadowed. If this is the case, try these remedies to counter the effects:

- Tape a calendar picture of nature with a good depth of view on the side of the towering object. When you get tired of working on family budgets, taxes, etc., the eye has a place to wander and a chance to relax. Looking at a picture with a good depth of field exercises the muscles of the eyes, reducing strain and stress.

- Hang or lean a mirror up against the structure, facing toward your workspace. The mirror will reflect the other side of the room or, if you are lucky enough to have a window opposite, it will reflect the light from that window, giving the feeling that the space is wider than it is.

9. Plants and flowers contribute to a more harmonious work environment and as you should already know by now, connect us with nature. Place one near or on your desk. Add a wind chime or miniature birdhouse to the planter. Use the wind chime as a symbol to signify a sale or an appointment you've just made. Running your fingers over the chimes can signify a benchmark reached in your day.

10. Use colors to augment your efforts. Color tips: Use some yellow for focus, beige for security, peach for a feeling of connectedness with others, deep blue or black for reflection, reds such as deep salmon or bright pinks for motivation, and green when you need to start a new project.

11. Create positive messages by displaying a prized award, certificate, or an inspirational quote.

12. Rejuvenate yourself with peppermint, jasmine, rosemary, or eucalyptus aromas when getting ready to tackle mentally challenging tasks such as doing your taxes or paying monthly bills.

13. Fix items that are broken—broken items send negative

messages. The desk chair with the broken leg may keep you and your work off balance. The clock running slow due to low battery power can keep you running late throughout your day. Tools that don't work clutter your workspace and can cause constant frustration when grabbing one by mistake.

14. If you stand in your workspace, make sure you have rubber pads beneath your feet to provide extra support and to protect your joints.

15. Symbols in your workspace should reflect the purpose of your activities. If you are a craft master, display some of your best work. A business in the home that produces the major income of the household should display symbols and items that reflect your credentials, promote motivation, and increase productivity.

16. Bring in Earth element accessories such as an earthenware bowl, textured stone paperweight, or square pencil box to provide groundedness.

17. Use a narrow, deep basket to hold important tax documents you receive between January and April tax time; the basket will be perfect for holding all sizes of forms and envelopes safely until April 15. Then when it's time to visit the accountant or tax preparer, all you need to do is pick up the basket and go.

18. A tip from one of our clients: Apply fabric to the wall or to metal cabinets using a cornstarch and water mixture as an adhesive. Cornstarch is not permanent and can be used as a temporary glue to adhere fabric, tissue paper, or other textured surface onto a wall or other object. This is a great remedy for walls that cannot be painted or when there are too many hard surfaces, such as file cabinets, in a space; the side of a refrigerator or a door that is unpleasant to look at cannot be changed or moved around in your space. When you move or want a change in your décor, just peel off the fabric. The cornstarch can easily be washed off the walls.

Chapter 15

The Quiet Rooms— The Bedroom and Bathroom

"The transformed place becomes our paradise as well, and in that world we're welcomed home."

—Albert Pinkham Ryder

HOW HECTIC IS YOUR LIFE? How many roles do you juggle? How challenged are you in your home life, career, or business? The twenty-first century has ushered in and wholeheartedly welcomed fast-paced living with stress as a companion. To compound this situation, we are bombarded by irritating noises, disturbing odors, movies that shock us, concert halls that rock us, and clutter that blocks us. Have you come up for air yet?

Take a deep breath as we take you on a mind excursion to comprehend the subtle power that the quiet rooms in your house have to address the challenges of your life on the go. These are the rooms where, within your home, you can create your own personal oasis, where you can start to unwind, slow down, and de-stress. Think of your bathroom and your bedroom as your getaway rooms, where you can remove yourself from your overworked, overstimulated, and overcommitted life. Here are some things to consider.

- Modern appliances make our housework easier but most families struggle to keep up with household chores due to busy schedules and mountains of *stuff*.
- Technology allows us to complete more work in less time, but many people are working longer hours than ever before.
- Because of computers and cell phones, instantaneous communication has become a right, not a privilege.
- More mothers work outside the home than ever before— then return home for what's been termed the second shift.

In order to maintain any semblance of a balanced and healthy life, you must start to deal with the plethora of stressors you encounter. Of course, there are many approaches to reducing stress, but none are so inexpensive and so absolutely necessary as addressing your rest and rejuvenation environments—the bedroom and the bathroom. Nothing does this so eloquently and effectively as feng shui. These are the rooms that should offer you a haven from not only your outside-of-home agenda but also inside-home activities and tasks—a place to shut the door and escape.

Here is the feng shui challenge we present: Start to rethink the bedroom and bathroom. The bedroom is not only a room where you sleep; it's also a room where you need to feel protected, embraced, and comforted. The bathroom isn't only functional; it's also a room where you need to feel soothed, refreshed, and relaxed. There's a reason some refer to this room as the *restroom*. Let's take a closer look at each of these rooms, using the Room Evaluators (see Chapter 10).

What Is the Function of the Bedroom?

You probably spend more time in the bedroom than any other room; after all, you sleep there. Being that you spend so much time in this room, it's important to know how the bedroom serves you. Give this some thought.

First of all, the focus of the bedroom should be on you, the individual, or, if a couple, the two of you as a couple. What you use, see, touch, hear, and otherwise experience should have meaning to you, not others. If you have children, don't display a lot of photos of them. The focus while in the bedroom should be on you, the couple, not you, the parents.

If you are finding that you are increasingly using the bedroom to do paperwork, watch TV, fold laundry, and exercise, then you are increasingly adding to your stress. The bedroom should not be a workroom; it is a room where you can relax, read, be romantic, have intimate conversations, listen to beautiful music, meditate, pray, do yoga, journal, think, and sleep. These are quiet activities that restore, recharge, and rejuvenate. Notice that yin produces yang: you rest and pamper yourself (yin) so that you feel invigorated (yang).

As much as we suggest that work be kept out of the bedroom, you may, due to a lack of space, have no place for a desk other than your bedroom. Here are a few tips for those of you in this situation:

- Use a screen to hide a desk when not in use.
- Keep papers, writing tools, etc., in boxes with lids. Take out what you need, then return the items to their designated boxes and cover with the lid.
- For the truly creative, cover the contents of the desktop by using a large box that has been trimmed and covered with fabric, wallpaper, or wrapping paper. Turn it upside down so that it fits over the desk. Another alternative to covering the box is to place a tablecloth over the box once you turn it upside down.

- Make a desk look less like a work desk and more like a place to write letters or work on a scrapbook or photo album. Start by covering the desk with a tablecloth or fabric that matches your bed linen and add a vase of real or silk flowers, tall blades of ornamental grass, feathers, or any other decorative items.
- If you have a large closet, remove the doors and sit the desk in a closet. Hang a curtain that can be opened and closed when needed.
- Try moving the desk to another room.
- Keep the desk clean when not in use and always cover the computer with an attractive piece of fabric.

Should the Bedroom Be More Yin or Yang?

Since the bedroom is a quiet room, it is considered to be more yin. Bright colors, complex patterns, and items that promote work *go against the nature* of the bedroom. One of the goals in feng shui is not to go against the nature of a person or a place. If a bedroom is too stimulating by using red, orange, and yellow as a color theme, too exciting due to loud, pulsating rock music, or too confusing due to various knickknack collections, then you've created an excess of yang, or a yin nightmare.

In the bedroom, a little yang goes a long way. For a feeling of cheerfulness, bring in some yellow flowers; to set the stage for romance, turn on some Barry White music.

Does the Room Look and Feel Balanced?

Ask the magic questions. Is the room top-heavy? Is it bottom-heavy? Is there too much furniture on one side of the room? As a reminder, we are not saying that it is wrong if you have a preference for items placed toward the top or bottom of your room. What we caution against is an obvious overload in any area of the room. If you rent or if you buy an existing house, some of these features are already in place. One such bedroom we saw came with big, heavy black ceiling beams against a white ceiling, six-inch dark wood ceiling molding, and a ceiling fan with wood blades. Nothing like a ceiling for a focal point!

Let your feng shui eyes come to your aid. As simple as it may seem, no other room needs to look and feel balanced more than the bedroom. A little tip: Some symmetrical balance goes a long way to creating a sense of equilibrium. Examples of this would be twin lamps or nightstands on each side of the bed.

Don't think because the bedroom has heavy or bulky furniture that it will be bottom-heavy. Headboards, dressers, a mirror placed or attached over a dresser, windows and window treatments are features that help balance the heaviness created by your large bed and other heavy furniture. If you find that your bedroom still seems bottom-heavy, try hanging items on the walls such as art, calendars, fans, a collage of postcards, and other decorative features.

Whether top-heavy, bottom-heavy, or lopsided, here are some other tips to create a more balanced look.

- Bring light to the side of the room that needs attention. If you don't have a place for a lamp, try using a light-colored tablecloth, place mat, or fabric.
- Lights directed up and hidden behind a nightstand or floor plant will take the eye up in a bottom-heavy room and a lamp with a sheer scarf over it will take the eye down.
- Try to use only bedroom furniture that you need; in the bedroom, less is more.

Does the Room Look Welcoming?

Sixty-three percent of Americans get less than the recommended eight hours of sleep per night, and many get less than seven hours. It's not hard to imagine that many of these people actually find their bedrooms uninviting. Here are some questions to ask yourself about the feel of the room:

- **What greets you as you enter the bedroom?** Stacks of books, piles of magazines, clothes on the floor? Or do your senses find a playground where you see the comfort offered by an uncluttered room, feel the texture of a throw, thrill in the quiet you hear, and smell the fresh air from an open window? Pay particular attention to what is beside your bed, because this is what you see before you turn out the lights. Chances are, if you see unfinished paperwork, books never read, or dirty dishes, your sleep will be negatively affected.
- **Are there items that look threatening?** Be careful of using large representations of predatory animals. The bedroom is also not the place for artwork depicting war, sadness, adverse weather, or any other negative theme.
- **Does the bedroom look too busy?** This one's important. Complexity negates your ability to achieve any semblance of a peaceful environment. If anything, err on the side of simplicity. The bedroom is not the place for large amounts of knickknacks, displays of collectibles, dolls, or toys. Of course, clutter is a big "no-no." Here's one you may not have thought about: electrical equipment. Keep this to a minimum due to electromagnetic fields that can harm you.

Are All Five Elements Present?

Good choices to use as the predominant element in the bedroom would be either Earth or Wood. Earth, of course, gives the room a feeling of stability, security, and discourages infidelity. So, if you need those influences in your bedroom, choose Earth as your predominant element.

Wood gives the room the feeling of adventure, change, and newness. If you need those influences, go with Wood as your predominant element.

Fire element is much too yang to use as the predominant element for such a yin room. Even so, a few splashes of Fire can be just what the doctor ordered when an influx of romance or passion is needed.

Be careful how you use Water in the bedroom. The colors of Water are dark blue and black. If you have a large amount of either of these colors, the bedroom will seem depressing. Swirls or wavy-patterned drapes or bedspread or a seaside print are more effective ways of incorporating the Water element into the bedroom.

Metal is also not a good element to use as a predominant element. If you refer back to Chapter 3, you will see that Metal conveys a message of endings, formality, ethics, and structure—not exactly the mood for the bedroom. Those of you who rent might find you are at the mercy of white walls and ceilings throughout your living space. If that's the case, here are some solutions to mitigate Metal in the bedroom.

- Choose the Earth element to reduce the oppressive Metal influence. Buttercream, beige, taupe, peach, or soft mocha would be great choices for bed linen. Ceramic plates, a bowl of interesting rocks, a landscape painting, or square pillows are other ways to bring in Earth.

- Fire melts Metal, so using a few Fire features will go a long way to controlling Metal in your bedroom. A candle with rocks arranged around the base of the candleholder makes for an excellent centerpiece for your dresser. A print of two lovers embracing or a red tassel tied around the top of the lamp base are clever Fire enhancements for the bedroom.

Good Placement in the Bedroom

The bed is the focal point for the bedroom, of course. The best position for your bed is the diagonal corner from the door of entry, so that you can see whoever enters. This is especially important for a child's room. Following is an illustration of a good position for the bed.

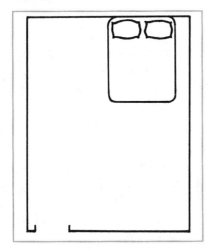

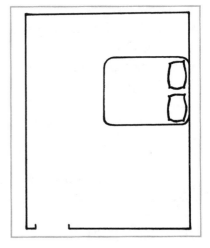

Good bed position: In this illustration the bed is diagonal from the entry with a clear view of those who might enter.

This is another good position for the bed, as it still allows you to see the entry.

Placing your bed directly in front of the entry with your feet facing the door places you in the most exposed and vulnerable position. It would be disturbing to allow those that pass by to see you in bed. In China, this is called the coffin position, because a deceased person's body could easily be removed from the room.

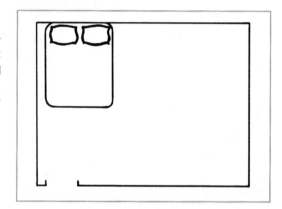

Bad bed position: In China, this is called the "coffin" position.

Avoid placing your bed under a sloped ceiling. The slope creates a squeezed feeling. If this can't be avoided, then drape soft fabric over the slope.

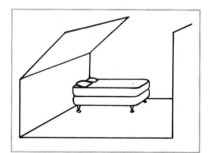

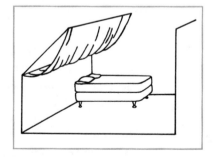

If you have no other option than to place your bed under a sloped ceiling, there is an easy remedy for it.

Sheer fabric, a sheet, lightweight curtains, or leftover fabric can be tacked or taped to the slope as shown in the illustration.

✳ Client Story: The Roommate Problem

Lucy shared an apartment with two other roommates. Her bedroom was the size of a large closet and the only place for her bed was directly in front of the door (coffin position). Her other bedroom furniture consisted of a nightstand that sat beside the bed, a dresser, and a small, two-shelf bookcase that sat side by side. On a tight budget, she called us, wondering if there was any solution to her problem. Even though she found it difficult to explain, she never liked having the bed where it was. When she read about the coffin position, it became imperative that the bed be moved. She was actually losing sleep over it.

Although the word *coffin* is alarming, we explained to her the reason why she never liked her bed in that position was that she was in the most vulnerable and exposed area of the room. Since she was right in front of the door, she was literally on display while she slept.

Rolling up our sleeves, we moved the small bookcase that was beside her dresser and sat it horizontally in front of the foot of her bed. Since it was not a tall item, it served as a barrier between her and the door while allowing her a view of the entry. We also took the silk plant that sat on her dresser and placed it on top of the shelf, as it would help camouflage her while still allowing a view of the door. Simple solutions are often the most effective.

She reported weeks later how much safer and relieved she felt. Just as important, she had no more sleepless nights.

Other Bad Bed Problems and How to Cure Them

It is best to have a solid wall behind your bed, as it provides a sense of protection and support. If it is impossible to have a solid wall and there are windows behind the bed, then create the illusion of a solid surface by closing the drapes or pulling down the shade before you get into bed.

It is best not to angle your bed so that it is diagonal to a corner; the triangle behind the bed that is formed by this positioning creates tension. If for some reason you must arrange it diagonally, place a lamp, a tall plant, or other such object in the triangle behind the bed, or drape some fabric across the corner in order to soften the space.

Be careful about placing a tall, heavy wardrobe or armoire too close to the front of the bed, especially if your bed sits low to the ground; anything that is large and imposing can make you feel diminished and overwhelmed. If you find yourself in this situation and cannot move the furniture, then be sure not to place any large item on top of the dresser. You can, however, mitigate the problem by bringing the eye down. You could place a real or silk plant with vines that fall down over the dresser or wardrobe. If you don't have a plant, you could place a tablecloth or fabric on the dresser so that the material hangs down over the sides. You could also use a gooseneck lamp and position the neck of the lamp downward; turn on the lamp to help take the eye down even more.

Mirrors in the Bedroom

A mirror should not be placed directly in front of bed; it can be startling to wake up in the morning and see yourself. Also, if you are nearsighted, the images you see in the mirror might frighten you as you lie in bed with only the moon to provide light. If you find that you have no other place for your dresser that has a mirror attached, then put a plant or other barrier in front of the mirror; it will deflect and camouflage whatever image is in the mirror.

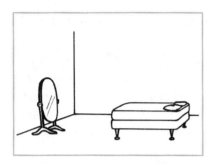

Don't place a mirror directly
in front of your bed.

Be careful not to place a mirror
in front of an entry door.

Don't place a mirror, especially a full-length one, on a wall or door directly opposite the entry door. The bedroom is meant to quiet and relax. Seeing yourself as you enter a bedroom can be too imposing. Whatever you see comes back to you immediately, and if you're tired, sick, or hurried, you'll only feel more so. And anyone coming into your bedroom for the first time will feel somewhat taken aback when they see a mirror at the bedroom entrance. It will put them on the spot, making them feel observed.

Tips for Bedrooms

1. If you want to add a little spice for romance, fold a red chenille throw and place it at the foot of your bed. Or depend on your lingerie to bring a yang influence when you need it.

2. Good colors for the bedroom would include soft greens, aqua, light mauve or rose, terra cotta, peach, buttercream, taupe, or beige. Don't think that you have to paint in order to bring in these colors. Think art, bed linen, pillows, place mats, napkins, and other items you may have on hand.

3. If you can see the bathroom from your bed, keep the bathroom door closed.

4. White walls abound in rental units. To mitigate those stark surfaces, try hanging your quilt instead of using it on your bed. You could also salvage last year's calendar featuring peaceful seascapes, gardens, or nature scenes; double-sided tape is all you need to mount three calendar prints on a foam core or on cardboard, and then onto the wall they go.

5. Refrain from keeping any collections in the bedroom, especially those of childlike items (applies to adults only).

6. Remove items that once belonged to former mates or spouses.

7. To add romance to your bedroom, check out the relationship sector of the bagua (see Chapter 5). Use artwork of a romantic theme, such as of a loving couple, lovebirds, turtledoves, hearts, quotations, and so on. Poetry books and romantic novels are great items to display in this area as well.

8. If you are single and you are looking for a meaningful relationship, keep a drawer empty and/or a little empty space in your closet. It sends a symbolic message that there is room in your life for another person.

9. Clear your clutter. Clutter destroys a relaxing atmosphere.

10. Besides sight, address the other senses. Some soothing scents include lavender, chamomile, ylang-ylang, and rose. Use a folded throw at the end of your bed for texture and play your favorite soothing music, such as acoustic guitar, soft classical music, or music that includes nature sounds. Set out a small bowl of lemon drops for a refreshing treat at the end of stressful day.

11. A less-desirable place for your bedroom is over a garage; these rooms tend to be colder in the winter and warmer in the summer. Also, the noise from the garage door is disturbing.

12. Your bed should look, feel, and smell inviting. By all means, make your bed every day.

13. Avoid using furniture or artwork with sharp edges or angles, as it appears aggressive.

14. The best place for a small child's bedroom is on the same floor as the parent.

Bathrooms

From a historical perspective, the bathroom is a fairly recent household phenomenon. It wasn't until the twentieth century that the bathroom was brought into the house as a standard room in the West. Because of this, no other room has demanded new feng shui recommendations more than the bathroom. What also has to be considered is that feng shui recommendations made in America will be different from those recommended in the East. Again, no way is right or wrong; what is important is what is appropriate for the particular culture based upon beliefs and long-held practices.

From a cultural perspective, Westerners adorn their bathrooms more than those in the East. Also, at least in America, bathrooms that are large are more preferred than smaller, as evidenced in new homes. It is also not uncommon for builders to eliminate a door between the master bedroom and master bathroom.

Bathrooms in Asia generally offer more of a sense of privacy than in the West. Not having a door on the bathroom would be considered bad feng shui. Placing the toilet in direct line of the bathroom entry door is very uncommon in China. The toilet often has its own separate room within the bathroom, or at least a separating partial wall to hide it. The master bathroom or any bathroom attached to a bedroom, a desired feature in American homes, would be seen as bad design and definitely bad feng shui in most Asian households.

In China, the bedroom is considered a very important and auspicious room, while the bathroom is considered a room of less status and importance. The bathroom is also a room where a draining, downward motion occurs as unsanitary water is carried away. Attaching the bedroom to a bathroom therefore conflicts with the high status of the bedroom. Some of this thinking comes from the sanitary conditions that used to exist in the East.

Good Feng Shui in Your Bathroom

More than any other room, the bathroom is your private space. You enter it in the morning with the expectation of leaving more refreshed and better looking than when you entered. Feng shui addresses more than just the mere functions of the bathroom; it strives to do the following:

- Make a utilitarian room a sensorial delight
- Reduce your stress level
- Help create a feeling of well-being

The bathroom offers amenities not found in any other room. Let's explore the possibilities.

What Is the Function of the Bathroom?

This should be a no-brainer. Basically, you clean and groom yourself. It is also the room for elimination. Hold on, there has to be more. Indeed, there is. In addition to the primary functions of the bathroom, this is the room that can relax, soothe, and slow you down. Try not to rush; take time to pamper yourself.

For centuries, bathing was part of social life and was an activity central to the core of society. These were places where you could be massaged, pampered, and socialize. The ancient tradition of Turkish baths and the importance of the sauna throughout the centuries in many Scandinavian and Austrian homes remind us of the important role that bathing played in everyday life. There's also a long history of bathing as a spiritual activity, such as the ritual washing of the feet from the Christian Bible and the mikveh, a ritual bath in Judaism.

Rethink the bathroom. This room can be a spa, relaxation center, and a health center all rolled up into one.

Should This Room Be More Yin or Yang?

Bathroom tasks are Water related. There is no other room that is so dominated by one element than the bathroom. You might say that the nature of the bathroom is ruled by Water. Since Water is the most yin of all the elements, the bathroom should have more of a yin influence. For this reason, be careful not to bring bright colors or bold, complex patterns into the bathroom.

Subtle yang features would be candles, burning of incense, a small vase of yellow flowers, or a radio to listen to as you shower.

Does the Bathroom Look and Feel Balanced?

Well, it's not like you can move the bathtub if one side of the room looks too heavy. Just a quick glance will tell you if you are keeping too many items on the floor, on your countertops, or around the top part of the room. Place baskets, plants, statues, or large trays filled with soap and lotion to bring some weight to the floor if necessary. To bring more attention to the top of the bathroom, apply a stencil around the top part of the room and hang art or other decorative items. Don't forget to use the top of the toilet tank as a display area; it brings attention to the middle of the room.

Does the Bathroom Look and Feel Welcoming?

As you enter this room, the overall look should say welcome—this is a place to relax and be pampered. For this reason, make sure the bathroom looks and smells fresh and sanitary. The rule of thumb for the bathroom is "clean and lean." You don't need to overdecorate this room but it shouldn't be boring either. A small dish of potpourri, some candles, or wind chimes near a window go a long way in creating a soothing environment. Choose appropriate colors for the bathroom as well. Here are some ideas.

- **Green**—it is a restful, healing color and also aids digestion. Soft, pastel shades are best. Refrain from using bright green, as it is too bold (yang).
- **Aqua**—this color derives its name from water.
- **Blue**—it is peaceful with a sedating effect.
- **White or ivory**—colors of cleanliness; they are also good colors for solo activity.
- **Gray or taupe**—these crisp and cool colors can appear sophisticated or masculine.

Does the Bathroom Look Busy?

Look to see where your toiletries are located. Have they expanded to shelves, counters, on top of the toilet tank? Are they blocking the mirror? Check the amount of electrical gadgets you are using. Be sure to put away your blow dryer and curling iron. Do you throw your dirty clothes and towels on the floor? Take a look inside medicine cabinets and closets that are in the bathroom. If you open these often, it is important that you *not* see old prescriptions, outdated aspirin, dried lotion, etc. If this is the case, you are giving preference to and making space for what is obsolete and worn out. Is that the message you want to give yourself?

Are All Five Elements Present?

In the bathroom, an abundance of Water surrounds you. With this in mind, following are ideas for bringing the elements into the bathroom:

- **Water**—use blue towels or bath mats, prints of fish, seashells, and other water motifs to correspond with the Water element that is inherently a part of the room.
- **Wood**—Water creates Wood according to the Creative Cycle, and using this element in the bathroom will make it feel harmonious and peaceful. Soft greens, aqua, wicker baskets, prints of trees or flowers, and striped wall-covering are great ways to incorporate the Wood element.
- **Fire**—just a few splashes of Fire is all you need in the bathroom. Use candles, incense, and soft rose as an accent color.
- **Earth**—ceramic tiles and soap dishes are common Earth features. Don't go overboard using Earth in the bathroom, as Earth dams Water, meaning that they oppose each other.
- **Metal**—this is a great element for the bathroom. Again, take a look at the Creative Cycle and you will see that Metal creates Water. These two elements work well together in the bathroom. Metal features such as white walls, metal-framed mirrors, metal towel bars, shower doors, or white towels make the bathroom look clean and crisp.

The Yin Side of Touch

Be aware that no sense takes as much prominence in the bathroom as that of touch. Most of the time your bathroom routine is so rote that you fail to relish the feel of warm water, the massage you give yourself when you wash your hair, and the texture you experience as you wrap yourself in a soft, cotton towel. Here is an exercise to help you benefit even more from your tactile experiences. This is a wonderful "slow you down" exercise. It is a "yin" ritual meant to prepare you for your daily work tasks (yang).

Choose one of your regular, everyday bathroom grooming or cleaning activities, such as combing your hair, applying lotion, washing your face, etc. As you start this task, close your eyes and concentrate on the whole experience. Go slower than usual and become aware of the motion or pattern. If you are using a scented product, smell the aroma. Do this for about thirty to forty-five seconds. Sound easy? The challenge lies in keeping your mind free of racing thoughts. Once you are successful in focusing on the task at hand, you will be amazed at the benefits.

Some Food for Thought

A word about the element of Water as it relates to the bathroom. The Chinese associate this element with prosperity and money and take countermeasures to address the fact that in the bathroom, water flows down and away from the dwelling. While cleanliness and health are paramount in feng shui, as Water is flushed away, money can be, too, metaphorically speaking. Here are some interesting "traditional" remedies that are used:

- Keep the toilet seat closed. You know, this is just a great idea because it demands that the guys close the lid. It also looks cleaner with the seat closed; the inside of a toilet is not particularly attractive.
- Bring in a few Earth element features (Earth dams Water) by using any ceramic item, a plate of rocks, a jar of pebbles, or brown, beige, tan, or peach colored items.

- Use plants that grow upward to counter the downward flow of water. This is a wonderful example of yin/yang balance.

Having offered these recommendations, we also want you to know that there is an advantage to having bathroom water flushed down the drain. To begin with, feng shui literally means "wind water." The ideal is to have wind and water that is clean and healthy, thereby benefiting humans.

Good ventilation and/or a window that opens can help provide for clean air (wind), while good plumbing assures you that the water used while in your bathroom, which is not clean, is taken away. If clean water represents good cash flow, then dirty water reflects the opposite.

Bathroom Tips

1. If you can see your bathroom from your bed, keep the bathroom door shut.
2. Decorate the bathroom to be relaxing and comfortable. Fold and stack towels so you can experience the texture, use baskets to hold bathing items, place candles around the bath tub, and play soft music or, better yet, bring out the CDs containing sounds of nature.
3. If you have no window in your bathroom, use a full-spectrum light bulb or the brightest bulb you can find.
4. Since the bath is a yin room, refrain from using too many yang features such as bold wall-covering patterns or bright colors. Instead choose wall covering with a small nature-themed pattern or swirls to mimic waves or water.
5. Use plants in the bathroom; they benefit from the warm and steamy atmosphere. It is also a good way to bring in the Wood element.

Chapter 16

Special Situations

Feng Shui for Entertaining
Feng Shui for Visitors
Feng Shui for Children's Spaces

"We can no longer separate ourselves from nature, nor can we ignore our impact on the world around us. By treating the body, mind and spirit with nature's own remedies, we bring harmony and balance to life."

—Christopher Day,
Architect

Feng Shui for Entertaining

Feng shui can help anyone create harmonious and beneficial energy for any social occasion, whether it is a dinner party, a business lunch, or a cocktail event. Specific seating and table shapes play pivotal roles when entertaining, as they can evoke different types of communication and interaction. Dashes of color, placement of seating, and pathways to and from the center of activities as well as knowing your guest's temperaments can ensure that your event is successful.

Specific communication styles and attitudes can be evoked during a social gathering based on proper application of feng shui. Feng shui principles help you determine the best seating arrangements as well as table shapes for your event. Here are some tips to generate given moods around a table or in a seating situation when entertaining.

Square—Earth Seating

The shape of a square connotes groundedness and security because of its equal proportions; thus, a square-shaped seating arrangement, or Earth seating, evokes a feeling of stability and respect for each person's participation. Only groups of four or eight persons can comfortably be seated in an Earth configuration. This shape is great when sharing meals with young children in a home. It keeps them focused and willing to share their day's events with the rest of the family. They also eat better because they feel safe. This seating style also tends to be more intimate for a dinner party and lends well to less-formal interaction and communication with guests.

Most dining tables are either rectangular or round, but this can be remedied. With a rectangular table, position a table runner and horizontal centerpiece at the center of the table to square it off, then position people to one side of the centerpiece. Just add square place mats to a round table.

If your table is long, create an intimate dining "nook" by placing a table runner and centerpiece so that you use a third of the table space.

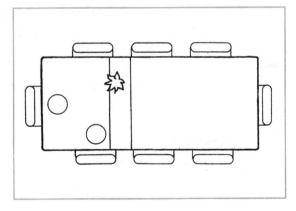

If you don't have a square table and want to create the square shape, follow these suggestions:

- Use square place mats
- Most napkins, both cloth and paper, are usually square shaped and can serve as inexpensive place mats.
- If two are dining at a square table, sit catty-cornered so you won't seem to be in opposition to one another.
- If you don't have a table at all and use TV trays, position them in the room so an implied square is visible.

Rectangle—Wood Seating

The rectangle is the Wood element shape in feng shui. Wood promotes exploration and new beginnings. The shape of a rectangle lends to lively conversation and adventure in trying new foods and recipes. If you entertain a lot of people during meals, the rectangular shaped table not only provides room for lots of people but also generates inquisitive and creative conversation. This table shape does not promote intimacy. If you don't have a rectangular table and want to promote this type of energy around the table, try these suggestions:

- Add an extension to your round or square table by pushing a sofa table against the dining table and cover both with a nice tablecloth or clean sheet. The sofa table will help to extend your dining space into a rectangular shape.
- When you have a need for a large rectangular table for holiday entertaining and no other resources are available within your home, it is not unheard of to borrow a long folding table from your church, work, or meeting hall along with chairs.

Our client Heather bought her first house and was eager to entertain a few of her friends. However, she did not have a kitchen table yet. She scoured her disheveled home with its unpacked boxes and mismatched end tables and night stands. After evaluating the resources in her inventory of furniture and boxes, she discovered that her two end tables and her nightstands were of the same height. Placing them end-to-end, she created a long narrow table. She then grabbed a heavy fabric-cutting board from her sewing supplies and placed it on top of the narrow end tables and nightstands. This created a wider surface on which to serve a meal while at the same time providing space underneath for people's legs once they sat down. Using a sheet for a tablecloth, she set the table with lightweight dishes, added candles and a small bouquet of flowers purchased from the grocery flower shop, and served a simple but elegant feast.

We know a couple who lived in an apartment above a drugstore. When they entertained, they would make a long dining table by taking their bedroom door off the hinges and placing it on top of two sawhorses borrowed from a friend. They covered the door with an heirloom tablecloth, placed candelabras on the table, lit the candles, and opened a bottle of wine, and they all sat down to a beautiful and tastefully prepared meal.

Round—Metal Seating

The circle is representative of the Metal element in feng shui. Round tables are great for conversation flow because no one person is seen as authoritarian. All guests can feel comfortable assuming responsibility for contributing to the conversation. This is a great shape for close friends to gather around to share good wine, good times, and to have fun. If this is the mood you wish to create and do not have a round table follow these suggestions:

- Use round place mats.
- Create this shape by piecing together two half circles cut from heavy cardboard; make the diameter the same as the length of the table you are covering. Using packing tape or duct tape, tape the two sides together to form a circle. Place the circle over the existing table and cover with tablecloth or other fabric.
- Using a table cover with a circular design will also work.

Irregular Shape—Water Seating

When entertaining a large group in your home, a random seating pattern works best. Random and nonspecific seating ensures heartfelt communications throughout the space. It also promotes meandering movement from one place to another. This is important when entertaining if you would like everyone to connect at some point during your event.

When planning for this type of seating pattern follow these guidelines:

- Make sure the path created by the seating arrangement is navigable and no seating blocks an entry.
- Arrange the seating to direct people naturally around the room but keeping focus on the heart or center of the activities.

Triangular—Fire Seating

In an entertainment situation, Fire seating is not the best situation. The reason is that the lone person at the point of the triangle, the isolated seat, ends up left out of the conversation or must carry the responsibility to control the conversation. However, an exception to that rule is a bartender on one side of the bar and two or more patrons conversing with the bartender. The bartender in this situation is vested with authority and is placed in the position of listener or advice giver.

To mitigate the triangle effect if three people are seated at a table, place an attractive centerpiece opposite the lone person sitting at the point of the triangle; this creates a "fourth" at the table. The more eye catching the centerpiece, the less obvious the triangle.

Octagon—Seating

The octagon shape is considered the most auspicious shape of the universe in feng shui.

You have both the circle and the square represented, assuring everyone equality, security, and balance in a communication situation. Octagon seating arrangements around a focal point in a room such as a fireplace are easy to arrange. Just draw an invisible line in your mind's eye when arranging chairs and tables, positioning each one at a point in the octagon. To represent an octagon shape at a table, create a display centerpiece that will imitate the eight-sided octagon or use octagon-shaped place mats. Bake an octagon-shaped cake. Use the main entrée when placed on the table as the center of the octagon and position other serving dishes, condiment bowls, etc., at each point of the octagon.

Engaging the Senses for Successful Entertaining

Smell

Smell, emotion, and memory are intimately linked in the limbic system of our bodies. There is no short-term memory with smell. When the olfactory bulb detects a scent, such as food, a lover, or a flower, it signals the brain and sends a message straight into the limbic system, crossing time and space barriers. This is why aromas play a big role in setting the mood for any occasion. Follow these guidelines for determining which aromas are best for your situation.

AROMA	REACTION
Vanilla	Triggers appetite; reduces stress
Floral smells	Promotes excitement and energy
Woody (cedar, sandalwood)	Softens mood in large gatherings (cedar wood is a good insect repellant for outdoor entertaining)
Musk	Sensuous; aphrodisiac
Cinnamon	Boosts heart and blood circulation and sexual urges
Clary Sage	Lifts depression
Lavender	Calms nervous tension
Citrus (lemons, grapefruit)	Refreshes tired minds

A good tip for using scents is to rub essential oil on cabinet edges, doorjambs, and drawer tracks that when moved will emit a subtle aroma each time.

Sight

In our culture today, sight has always been the most emphasized of the senses. In an entertaining situation, engaging this sense can be done through two approaches:

1. Use light to set the mood of the room.
   - Candles
   - Lighting directed up, set behind plants and furniture
   - Dim the overhead lights

2. Bring colors in for the occasion.
    - Terra-cotta and peach colors are good for connecting in conversation. Bring these colors in through napkins, tablecloths, your clothing, flower arrangements, and food presentation.
    - Red is a good color to make people salivate and eat well. Add touches of this color with red candles, napkins, plates, red wine, or red seat covers.
    - Greens and blues calm and soothe the eye. Once again, choose table settings and place mats, candles, or other accessories that display these colors.
    - Yellow makes cheerful and warm feelings emanate. Don't use too much of this color, however. Try punches of it in a flower arrangement or food display.

Sound

The most musical and poetic of the senses is the sense of hearing. Animate your social event by turning it into a song. The age group of your audience determines the sounds you choose to bring in to inspire, motivate, and entertain.

- Play favorite music of those who are invited. Infusing soft classical or baroque music of past eras as guests arrive at your threshold might set the mood for a more demure cocktail event. For an event with a '50s, '70s, or '80s theme, it would be more fitting to play songs from those eras. Adjust volume to the appropriate level to allow for conversation.
- For intimate entertaining where only two people are present, romantic music, sounds of ocean waves, nature, thunderstorms, a crackling fire, and even the sound of

brewing coffee or of wine being uncorked and poured into glasses all set a mood.

- Use outdoor items indoors. Bring in chimes, placing them where people can run their fingers over them as they pass by.

Touch

Humans can survive without hearing, sight, smell, and even without the pleasures of taste. But without touch, we cannot survive psychologically. Always invite touch through textures in your feng shui entertaining. The formula for creating comfort zones in a space for guests is easy.

- Ensure guests have a comfortable place to sit.
- Provide small pillows for deep chairs and couches to accommodate smaller people who don't want to look silly sitting while their feet hang above the floor.
- Balance out feminine and masculine textures for a mixed-gender event. Feminine usually implies frilly, lacy, soft, and cushiony, while masculine usually implies smooth, straight lines, leather, and more tactile textures like chenille, berber, and wood.
- During your event, bring out special pieces in a collection that entice people to pick up and examine them. (Doing this can provide an icebreaker for those less inclined to initiate conversation for fear of not knowing the correct thing to talk about. Steering the conversation to the object takes away that fear.)

Taste

This is our most festive sense—the party sense. Taste, laughter, good food, and gatherings of good friends and family come to mind. The sense of taste in entertaining is all about pleasing others. Engage a taste sensorial adventure for your guests.

- Put some consumable item in each room that your guests might visit to tickle this sensorial element. Chocolates, mints, nuts, relish trays, chips and dip entice the taste buds.
- Brew orange or lemon peels in a small pan on the stove releasing their marvelous aromas.
- Simmer cinnamon sticks, nutmeg, and cardamom or vanilla in a pot on the stove. Research has shown that men are especially attracted to food scents. Also, these aromas increase appetite and a festive feeling.

Hosting Overnight Visitors

The mere thought of having an overnight guest can petrify many of us. Still, there are those who love to host a visitor to their home. There is a medley of tips to help you make your guest feel comfortable and welcomed:

- Give them a space they can call their own while they are in your home.
- Provide them with a basket of essentials such as soap, shampoo, toothpaste, toothbrush, body lotions, and other amenities. Many people save samples from hotels or you can pick up travel sizes at any drugstore. We save samples that come in the mail for these types of situations. Make sure baskets for male guests contain shaving items.
- If the guest is a family member, place framed pictures of fun family memories on a nightstand in the room where they will be sleeping. This gives them a Tao connection, as talked about in Chapter 2.

- Provide an empty frame so they can put their own picture on the nightstand.
- Infuse an aroma you know will comfort the visitor based on information mentioned in this book regarding the sense of smell. Rose is a wonderful aroma that many women love; lavender is calming; men usually like more woody aromas; and so on.
- Place your best towels and face cloths where your guest can see them, either at the foot of the bed or on the bathroom counter or hung over the tub.
- Have a nightlight in the bedroom or bathroom to assist the visitor who gets up at night to visit the bathroom. This helps them get their bearings to know where to go if they've not stayed with you before.
- If the bedroom or bathroom has space, provide a small coffee pot or miniature plug-in teapot along with cups, coffee and/or tea, and packets of sweetener and powdered cream. This is a nice homey touch that allows your guests to make their own coffee or tea if they arise before you get up in the morning.
- Providing tactile experiences for your guests will make their time in your home a pleasant one. If possible, place a thick fluffy rug that their feet will connect with as they step down from the bed. Provide extra bed pillows in case they want to read in bed.
- A lamp with a three-way bulb allows the guest to control the light in the room—low wattage for watching television or moving around the room, and higher wattages for reading or task-oriented activities.
- A telephone and telephone book in the room also lends to the guest's feeling of independence in your home. A hand-written or typed list of important numbers such

as police, fire, or a good restaurant may come in handy as well.

- Instructions to your guest about the general habits of any pets in the home is always appreciated. Walking through a home at night after others are in bed, a guest can be startled by the sudden appearance of a growling or barking dog or a cat that likes to sneak up and surprise those walking through a room.

Put yourself in the shoes of your visitor. How would you like to be treated when visiting another's home? Learn from bad experiences you have had to prevent your guests from experiencing the same.

Child's Play

Applying feng shui to children's spaces is fun because adults are able to bring out the child in themselves without fear of judgment from others. Children are famous for improvising with anything available. They don't always use or consume what is selected for them to play with, wear, or eat. Keep that in mind when using feng shui for your child.

Create spaces that allow their imaginations to soar, their self-esteem to stay intact, and that guarantee their feeling of safety and security. Many times parents will place a large, looming dresser in a child's room. Having such a large piece of furniture towering over a bed or play area can make a child feel uncomfortable and insecure.

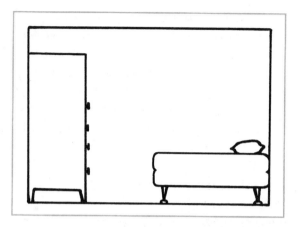

Placing a tall dresser
in front of a child's
bed can overwhelm
or intimidate a child.

Children experience their environment much more strongly through their senses than do adults, as they are more receptive. They trust and are open to all experiences until they identify on their own terms what nurtures them and what doesn't. These are the areas that should be addressed:

1. Allow a child space where she or he can build a makeshift tent using chairs, couches, and cushions. Just like adults, children like time away from others but also want to feel safe and close to mom and dad. The tent enclosure provides the refuge while still separating their play space from others.

2. Containerizing their arts and crafts supplies in small shoe bags, plastic tubs, or other easy-to-open boxes and cans allows them to access their crayons and drawing pads without having to wait for an adult to lift or open them. The smaller the containers, the easier it is for children to carry and open them. Doing this gives them a feeling of independence.

3. Small children's storage bins should be low to the floor.

No storage that they would need to access should be above their arms' reach, in order to prevent them from toppling shelves or dressers should they attempt to climb up on them to get an item.

4. Hanging pictures at eye level brings the world to their level. Take this fact into consideration with babies in cribs. Their eye focus develops in stages as they grow. Pictures and decorative objects on the wall should be moved to the baby's eye level if they are meant to stimulate the baby while she or he is lying in the crib. Otherwise the baby will never connect with them.

5. Children of every age should be presented with opportunities at every turn to have a sensorial experience. After all, it is at this time in their lives when childhood memories are created that will surface in adulthood when similar sensorial experiences are present.

   • **Touch**—Bring in soft, plushy items for children to cuddle; smooth, silky textures (satin fabrics) for coolness; and thick, nubbly textures (chenille or wool blankets) for warmth.

   Take them out into nature during the warm summer months and let them run barefoot to connect naturally with the earth, pebbles, grass, and water.

   • **Sight**—Children respond wonderfully to color stimulation. Infants do not see color during the early months of their development but do respond to contrasts. Black and white toys provide this. Research has shown that as children grow, the primary colors play a prominent role in their development. Through the toddler years, bring in these colors on blankets, toys, and clothing. Children are invigorated by sunlight and, conversely, need darkness to sleep well. To control sleep time, use room-darkening shades for naptime.

Make sure that the artwork in the child's room is not scary, threatening, or dreary. Instead use art that looks fun as seen in a favorite cartoon character poster and inspirational in a print of a hero or heroine. Don't forget to use the child's awards or trophies, art work created by the child, or favorite vacation photos.

- **Sound**—Nature sounds delight children but can sometimes scare them. Sounds to educate little ones can easily be incorporated into a child's space through toys.

- **Smell and taste**—Bake cookies! Create memories for your child through kitchen aromas. Go to the state fair and eat cotton candy. One of our favorite memories from childhood is the smell of a brand-new baby doll under the Christmas tree.

Children's spaces encompass the world outside. Don't keep them cooped up inside in manmade environments. Experience the world with them. Become a child yourself and bask in the sensorial experiences you have forgotten.

Section IV
Learning by Example

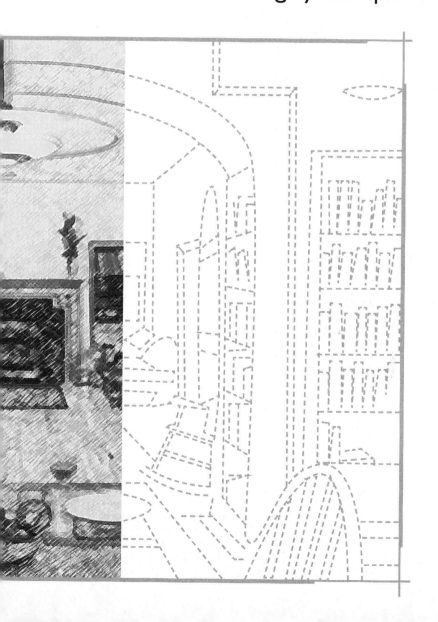

Chapter 17

A Cure for Whatever Ails You

"Health is the greatest gift, contentment the greatest wealth, faithfulness the best relationship."

—Buddha

AS WE HAVE SO often mentioned, feng shui is not just about moving furniture. It's about creating a better life for yourself and for your family. Want to improve yourself, your finances, health, relationships, or career or professional situation? Feng shui can help.

Feng shui is not meant to be the one "cure all." If you want to make a career change, you may also need to take few classes or finish that degree. If you want to meet new people, maybe you should join a ski club, take a dance class, or get active in a church social group. If you want to improve your finances, you may need to educate yourself about investments.

If you do your part, feng shui will do its part. To some, feng shui solutions are so immediate and astonishing that it almost appears magical. To others, the remedies seem so logical or grounded in common sense that they wonder how they did not think of the solution themselves. No matter what you think, we want you to know that feng shui can help guide, motivate, inspire, and nurture you in your quest for a more fulfilling life.

Okay, you say, so you believe in the benefits of feng shui but you want to know specifically how feng shui can help you find a companion, change your career, or whatever it is your heart desires. Let's take a look at common life situations or problems posed to us in workshops and during consultations; maybe you will relate to one or two or all of these situations.

1. *I can't seem to keep an intimate relationship in my life. What can I do to change that?*

   - Check the relationship corners of your rooms for symbols that represent "one" and replace any with two or more of something. For instance, replace a picture of a single rose with a bouquet of flowers, two mourning doves, or a live plant that blooms regularly to signify longevity. Never leave a relationship corner empty.
   - If you want another to enter your life, then you symbolically need to make room for another. Clear a space in your closet and at least one dresser drawer.
   - If your bedroom has room, place two chairs side by side in the relationship corner. Turn on a light or light a candle in the wisdom/knowledge corner to activate wisdom in your choice of a mate.

2. *I have had an estranged relationship from my family for years and wish to rekindle my ties. What can I do in order to reconnect with my family?*

   - Do this gradually. Place the pictures of your estranged family members in a bedroom dresser drawer. Pull them out every morning and take a look at them; just as you start your day with them in mind, you can also start a new relationship with them. In a few weeks, place the photos on your dresser or in your family room; now you are giving more attention to them. The next step is yours to take. Call the family member(s) and bury the hatchet.

- Activate the compassion/helpful people corner using a symbol such as a lamp or spiritual quote; just as you are committing time and effort to this important endeavor, you can't do this alone. If you make the effort, you will need your family members to do the same as well.
- Activate the wisdom/knowledge corner with a Metal element feature to remind you to let go of the old and make way for the eventual connection with estranged family members.

3. *I am new at my job and want to be accepted by my coworkers. How can I change my workspace to invite friendship?*

- Often you can change the impression you make on others by reorganizing your workstation. If your back faces your coworkers, strategically place a mirror or other reflective object so you can see them approach. This will give you more control over your interactions with peers.
- Don't be a clutter bug. Keep your workspace clean. Always make sure chairs are not stacked with paper or boxes so that when someone visits, they have a comfortable place to sit.
- Place a silk or live plant on your desk; people are natu-

rally attracted to nature. If possible, use a floor plant with a small fan hidden behind it. Turn the fan on low when a coworker visits. This will imitate a breeze and seem refreshing to your visitor.

- Want your space to feel welcoming? Say it with a welcome plaque or place a bowl of candy by an empty chair.
- Decorate your office/workspace for each season, inviting others to come in and experience them. Be a gracious host/hostess in your office space.

4. *I'm having trouble sticking to my exercise program, which I do at home.*

- Bring the Fire element into the space where you do it. Add a punch of red by using a red yoga ball or red towel.
- Infuse aromas such as citrus or green apple to inspire you and to uplift the spirit.
- If you have a window in the room, position the equipment to face the window. Views of nature are always beneficial.
- Bring in plants to connect with nature.
- Hang inspirational pictures and posters to cheer you on as you exercise.
- Play salsa or other upbeat music while you exercise.

5. *I want to lose weight. I've tried over and over again with no success. Any suggestions?*

- Blue suppresses the appetite, so try to get blue into the space where you eat, whether through plates, place mats, or wall hangings.

- Remove pictures and magnets representing any kind of fattening food from your refrigerator.
- Use a small easel to place a cookbook that has a picture of a colorful, healthy meal on its cover.
- Save your carbs for the evening (yin), as they slow you down.

6. *I have insomnia. What can I do to get some sleep?*

- Spend more time out of doors where the body can soak up the sunlight, which is good for circadian rhythms. Also check your bedroom for reminders of work and remove or camouflage them. Play soft music as you lie in bed. Make sure you eliminate any artificial light and keep to the natural glow of the moon.
- Maybe your room lacks good air circulation and as a result the room feels stuffy or stale. If you have a ceiling fan, turn it on to keep air circulating; if you don't have a ceiling fan, any quiet fan will do.
- Maybe your room is too dry in the winter. Fill a pretty bowl with water and place it by the heat register to send moisture into the air. Run hot water in the shower for a few minutes to send moisture into the air or fill the tub with water and let it sit overnight while you sleep. Some of the water will evaporate into the air, alleviating some of the dryness.
- Remove pieces of furniture that seem to loom over you as you sleep. This could make you feel oppressed and uneasy, thus preventing sleep from coming to you.
- Don't put the computer or television where you can see it from the bed, as these can be distractions.
- Sometimes buzzing noises from outside a window

caused by electrical transformers or traffic noises throughout the night can be irritating. Turn on a small fan close to your bed to create a white noise that will help drown out the irritating sound.
- Music that has been shown to induce sleep includes Debussy's "Ondine" or Bach's "Goldberg Variations."

7. *I earn a good living but I can't seem to hold on to my money. It's like money comes in one door and goes out the other. I've had this problem most of my life.*

- Sounds like we're really talking about a need for stability, so bring the Earth element into your environment. The Earth element represents stability and good money handling.
- Architectural features that suggest quick entry and exit may be a problem, such as two doors directly opposite each other or a straight hallway without features that slow down the eye. Place an item between the two doors or hang alternating wall decorations along the hallway.
- If you have burdensome debt, look out for unnecessary papers, files, magazines, clothes, or household items.
- As this book suggests, start using what you have! Stop buying another white shirt or blouse if you already have three of them. Focus on possessions that are meaningful or serve a purpose; discipline yourself by not buying more than you need or already have.
- After you clear your clutter, have a garage sale and start earning money from your stuff. Bet you didn't know you had money staring you right in the face!

8. *I've been working for a company for two years and am anxious for a promotion. How can I position myself for a promotion and raise?*

- Place a few awards along with your credentials in your workspace; if you want people to notice you, give them something to take note of. Don't go overboard, because you may seem boastful.
- If you want to promote your specific attributes, look to the elements. Want to appear focused and detail oriented? Place a metal paperweight on your desk and keep your office organized. Want to appear innovative? Bring in the Wood element by using plants and rectangular objects. Want to instill trust? Let Earth come to the rescue. Try a beige or brown desk mat.
- Raise your chair to a higher position so that you physically look elevated.
- Add a Water feature such as a fountain, glass object, etc., in your self/career station at home to symbolize a clear flow of opportunities in your job.

9. *I live in an apartment on the twentieth floor. I miss living in a house. Any ideas?*

- First and foremost, bring nature into your apartment. Go on an expedition in a nearby park, beach, or any outdoor area and collect indigenous items. Rocks, pinecones, seashells, or wild flowers are excellent materials to use for homemade decorations. Fill a glass bowl with any one of these items to help connect you to nature.
- Bring in plants and garden features to imitate a small garden. If your space is limited, create your indoor

garden on a small table; if you have lots of light and space, you could actually set aside space for an indoor garden retreat.

- In some apartments, the living and dining rooms share one common area. If this is the case, create a separation between these two areas. It will feel like you have two rooms. You can do this by placing a screen between the two areas. If you don't have a screen, hang fabric or use a row of plants as your separator. Bookcases that are flush against the wall might be put to better use as the physical boundary separating these two areas.

- Change the faceplate on light switches and outlets, covering them with decorative wallpaper, paint, or fabric. Also hanging a mirror or picture over the electrical box hides the obvious. Painting the doorknocker and ringer/peephole plate a bright yellow or other inspiring color can differentiate your door from all the other mundane ones on the floor.

- If you live in a large loft apartment where everything is in one big open area, your challenge is a bit more troublesome. Create a cozy intimate space for reading or watching television by stringing wire or strong rope around the area you wish to create. Hang decorative cloth over the rope. If you have heavy chains and hooks available, hang old windows and doors from the ceiling to create separate spaces. If you are an artist, hang paintings from these hooks to create your own personal art gallery.

10. *I'm a divorced parent with a shy child who visits me regularly on the weekends. I want to create a space that will be nurturing,*

cozy, and fun but that will also make my child feel secure. I'm a
renter, so I can't make drastic changes. What do you suggest?

• Create a place that affords both discovery and security
  when planning a child's space. A skirted table, crawl-
  through tubing, or a tent made with sheets offer a
  small child opportunities for exploring and finding
  refuge where he or she can curl up with a favorite toy
  or book.
• A child who is shy may need a few extra comforts in
  his or her bedroom such as a soft throw or blanket,
  some small bed pillows, or stuffed animals.
• Place a few protective symbols in your space. Small
  children look to their parents as their first line of protection, so make sure there is a photo of both parents
  in the room. This is especially important in the case of
  a divorce; if this is the case, make sure there's a picture
  of your former spouse in your child's room. Statues of
  angels can be protective, too.
• Furniture in the room should relate to the size of your
  child, and pictures and hooks should be hung lower
  than usual to accommodate the eye level of the child.

Chapter 18

Clients Who Used What They Had

"An understanding of feng shui offers a more systematic or scientific way the desire for change can be applied."

—George Birdsall

Too Much of Him in Her Room

Betty was recently divorced. Her sadness and despondency were quite evident. She lived in the same house with her husband for more than twelve years, which made it difficult to sever memories of a marriage gone wrong. Betty wanted to feel happy in her home. As it was, she and her home looked gloomy. "Even though he is gone I feel like he is still here," Betty told us. Her words echoed a Pyramid feng shui belief that our dwellings mirror our inner selves.

When we arrived, the first room Betty showed us was her bedroom. We discovered the following:

- Two of the four drawers in her dresser were filled with her ex-husband's clothes, some of the bookshelves were filled with his books, and several pieces of art that belonged to him still hung in the room.
- Several pieces of bedroom furniture belonged to her ex.

- The bedroom was painted a muted, drab olive green.
- Her bed was placed almost directly in front of the door.
- Clutter had become a decorative feature.

Even though there were several sore spots in her house that needed attention, this room was the main culprit. We made the following suggestions:

- Remove the ex-husband's furniture and belongings. Since her ex-husband didn't want these items, she sold them.
- Reposition the bed so that it is in the empowerment/wealth corner, which is the most diagonal corner from the door of entry. This position also allowed for her bed to be against a solid wall, reducing the feeling of vulnerability.
- Carefully sort through *her* books, objects, and artwork; choose items she considered meaningful, and remove the rest.
- Use water or ocean scenes to remind her of her favorite place and decrease the depressing aspect of the walls.

The reward was the immediate pleasure she experienced in her newly arranged haven. As she eliminated items that once belonged to her husband along with items that no longer served her, she symbolically severed the final bonds that held her captive to painful and unpleasant memories.

The icing on the cake came from her four-year-old son, who exclaimed, "Mommy, your room is the most *beautifulest* room. I want my bedroom to be like yours." The woman who had been melancholic was now cheerful and bubbly. Betty sent us a lovely thank-you card in which she wrote: "I couldn't have predicted that in all that grief I was handling over the end of my marriage, I and my child would emerge so much happier."

Stuck in His Ways

Gary's ex-girlfriend had left him because she felt that he was too rigid and stuck in his ways, but now he was anxious to meet the love of his life. We understood just how entrenched his behavior was by the outward symbols within his home:

- Posters of mixed-drink formulas decorated his dining room.
- A huge clock that hung on the wall was the first thing to greet visitors upon entry.
- The living room furniture was positioned in a very symmetrical pattern, with a couch in the middle of a wall flanked by two coffee tables on each end. Two matching chairs were set perpendicular at each arm.

After we explained that the drink formulas stressed "following instructions," Gary replaced the posters with a print of a French café that had been in storage. He also moved the clock to a less conspicuous wall, removing the emphasis on punctuality.

We rearranged the living room furniture on a diagonal and placed the two chairs beside each other, separating them with one of the coffee tables.

Gary called us a few months later for some follow-up advice and told us that he was really enjoying his newly arranged space. He also added, "I have to admit, I felt really uncomfortable with the changes and wanted to put everything back but I didn't because what you pointed out to me made so much sense." It took him three weeks to start to relax and feel comfortable with the changes.

One year later, Gary called to request a feng shui consultation for his new house. Seems Gary got a promotion at work *and* had met the love of his life.

Help! I Can't Breathe!

Karen and Jerry attended a feng shui "prosperity" workshop we gave. We asked our audience to write down one word that would describe how they felt about their current financial situation. Spouses were not to share with each other. Following these directions, both Karen and Jerry amazingly wrote down the same word, *smothered.*

At the break Karen confided in us that she and Jerry filed bankruptcy recently. She had been on total disability for five years due to severe chronic asthma. Karen had worked as a respiratory therapist for twenty years, although she'd always disliked it. She had always felt smothered because it was a career choice made for her by her parents.

During the workshop, Jerry had been ribbing Karen about her books. It turned out books from her professional training and medical texts related to her job had overrun the house. She was keeping the books in case she needed them again someday.

We knew these books were symbols of the more than twenty years Karen had worked in a job she hated. Most of the materials in her medical books were obsolete, as new technology had changed the field so much. They were serving no useful purpose for her. It just never occurred to Karen to get rid of them.

Six months after the seminar, Karen called to let us know she threw away most of her outdated books and donated the others to the medical library at her alma mater. Karen had been able to go back to work due to a miraculous turnaround with her asthma. Now, both Jerry and Karen are working good jobs doing what they like.

Once she let go of the possessions that were smothering her, Karen found she had room for new opportunities and miraculously, the air became easier to breathe. Vitality entered their lives and prosperity was within reach once again.

The Invisible Woman

Marci was a young career woman who didn't feel as if she was moving forward as quickly as she could in her career. The boss never acknowledged her contributions to team projects. She felt invisible to her superiors. Our assessment of her environment proved revealing, as we noticed numerous pictures of translucent, solitary women facing away.

We suggested she eliminate some of these pieces and add pictures or symbols representing team spirit, making sure the symbols included women in leadership roles or showed other activities that embodied self-empowerment. The frames that had held the prints of the invisible women could hold certificates, diplomas, or any other credentials reminding her of her capabilities. The books and trade magazines she owned in her field of expertise were hidden away. We suggested she display these for easy referral.

Marci did as we recommended and the results were startling. She shared that she hadn't realized how depressed she had been until she realized how positive and up she had become. This became evident to her as her coworkers and boss commented on her new attitude. As her attitude changed, so did her productivity. Three months later, she received a promotion.

A Feng Shui Mother Knows Best

A fellow practitioner shared this story with us about her daughter. Heidi, who was attending her last year of college, called home in a panic: "I have to write an article for the college newspaper and my research paper for my marketing class is due tomorrow. My mind feels cluttered with everything that has been going on this week. Everybody wants my attention. The dog is waiting for his walk, the cat is screaming to be fed, and the telemarketers keep calling to sell me long-distance service! I can't find the top of my desk, and somewhere under all of these reference books and rough drafts is my computer."

Our feng shui mother had a hunch about the real problem immediately. Heidi shared an apartment with another student. Both she and her roommate had busy schedules and neither had time to stay on top of the clutter accumulating around them. Finals were fast approaching and the stress was beginning to stifle any creativity she had.

This feng shui mother leaned back in her chair and gave out age-old secret feng shui advice: "Clean your room!" Of course, Heidi didn't like hearing that. But Mom asked her to imagine that her workspace was her mind. Then she asked her to describe her mind.

Slowly Heidi became aware that her desk and her mind looked the same: covered in clutter. Later that week, she called to report that after the mother-daughter conversation she was able to complete both projects on time and that the article for the newspaper was one of the best she had ever written.

Feng shui is a metaphor for living and Heidi learned two new things that evening:

1. That connecting with her immediate environment, in whatever condition, is mirrored in her mind. Therefore, to keep her mind uncluttered, she must keep her surroundings uncluttered.
2. That Mom is a person of great wisdom!

The next time you are having a problem focusing, clear out some clutter. Free up some space. Make room for creativity!

Missing Her Garden

Last year we met with Tessie, a senior citizen and avid gardener. Tessie sold her home earlier than expected and ended up moving into a townhouse apartment for a year. She would eventually move in with her daughter and son-in-law when her daughter's job transfer was complete and their new home was built. The new home would have space for her gardening, so while she lived in the townhouse she stored much of her garden art and sculptures.

Our client was unhappy and depressed because she couldn't garden every day. She longed for her garden and continually imagined herself walking through her gate and connecting with the abundance of mother earth. Living in this apartment removed her from her familiar daily routine and time spent planting, pruning, and harvesting her garden. She no longer could experience the cycles of the seasons, which she so enjoyed.

We suggested she take some of her garden items out of storage and use them in her apartment to provide her with the connection with nature she missed. She had a small garden arbor that fit perfectly over the apartment front door and would cover the outside landing. Getting permission from the property manager, we helped her position the arbor outside over the door.

Our client's front door now has the same effect as her garden gate, connecting her to what she loves most. She no longer feels lonely, depressed, or cut off from her passion.

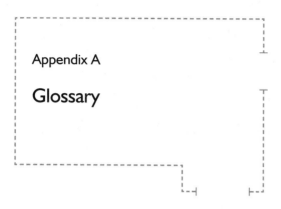

Appendix A

Glossary

Aromatherapy:

The study of therapeutic uses of essential oils. Feng shui is mainly concerned with the application of essential oils through the sense of smell (inhalation).

Bagua:

A geometric shape, either an octagon or a tic-tac-toe grid, used to locate the important "stations" within a room, house, or garden. The stations include: Self/Career, Wisdom/Knowledge, Community/Elders, Empowerment/Wealth, Future/Fame, Relationships/Marriage, Legacy/Children, Compassion/Helpful People, and Health.

Bau biologie:

The study of the impact of building materials upon the health of people and the application of this knowledge to the construction of healthy homes and work places; the science of holistic interactions between life and living environment.

Biophilia hypothesis:

Introduced by E.O. Wilson, it states a common theme shared by all environmental studies in that humans have a natural affinity to nature. We are genetically encoded so that our connection to nature is engrained in our whole psyche and being.

Black Hat Sect Feng Shui:

Founded by Professor Lin Yun, this is considered the first Western approach to feng shui; this school orients the bagua according to the position of the entrance door.

Black Tortoise:

One of the four protective animals; it is associated with the north and the Water element. It is positioned in the back of a dwelling or structure.

Chi:

Often referred to as the breath of life or the vitality of a space. According to traditional Chinese feng shui, this is an invisible life force or energy in and around our bodies and environments. We experience chi through our senses—what we see, smell, hear, touch, and taste, as well as through what we don't see, smell, hear, touch, or taste.

Community/Elders:

Area of the bagua that represents the gifts, talents, and wisdom bestowed on you by others who have gone before you—those who provide guidance, leadership, strength, and direction. In traditional Chinese feng shui, this area is located east; in Western feng shui, it is the middle area of the left side of the room.

Compass School:

This school of feng shui uses the compass to find auspicious directions according to a person's birth date. This school introduced the yin/yang and the five element theories.

Compassion/Helpful People:

Area of the bagua that represents both the bounty bestowed upon you and the compassion you show to others. In traditional Chinese feng shui, this area is located northwest; in Western feng shui it is the lower right corner of the room.

Cure:

A feng shui recommendation meant to bring about desired change.

Creative Cycle:

Cycle of harmony in which elements create the next element in a forward, clockwise motion. Wood creates Fire, Fire creates Earth, Earth creates Metal, Metal creates Water, and Water creates Wood.

Destruction Cycle:

Cycle in which the elements have the power to control or destroy one another. Wood takes from Earth, Earth dams Water, Water puts out Fire, Fire melts Metal, Metal chops Wood.

Earth:

One of the five elements, it includes the following characteristics: Square, center, terra cotta, earth tones/ browns, sand tones/ gray. It represents humanity, safety, and security.

East:

This direction is associated with the Wood element and represents creation, upward growth, change, new beginnings, flexible thinking, and nourishment.

Ecopsychology:

A school within the field of psychology that holds that human nature and behavior are affected by an inherent bond to the earth and natural environment.

Empowerment/Wealth:

Area of the bagua that represents abundance and empowerment. In traditional Chinese feng shui, this area is located southeast; in Western feng shui, it is the left upper corner of the room.

Feng shui:

An art and science that helps us live in harmony with our surroundings. Feng shui looks to nature as a guide, and is the study of person/place connection as well as a means to protect, heal, and restore.

Fire:

One of the five elements, it includes the following characteristics: Triangle, south, and red tones. It represents action, intellectual growth, and life's productivity.

Five Element Theory:

An integral concept of Chinese philosophy, it states that the elements Wood, Fire, Earth, Metal, and Water are the building blocks of the universe. These elements interact with each other and it is crucial that they not be seen as fixed or separate.

Five senses:

Includes touch, sight, smell, sound, and taste, which are all used to continually process messages from our environment.

Form School:

Considered the first school of feng shui; it focuses on topography of the land.

Future/Fame:

Area of the bagua that represents the bringing about of clarity and vision for your goals and aspirations, and how you want the world to know you. In traditional Chinese feng shui, this area is located south; in Western feng shui, it is the upper middle area of the room.

Geomancy:

Ancient holistic science of living in harmony with the earth; the art of finding the right place and time for any human activity. This science regards the earth as a conscious living being and considers all forms of life as interconnected.

Goal:

Specific objective that can be defined in terms of action, time line, and outcome.

Green Dragon:

One of the four protective animals; it represents the east and the Wood element. It is located on the left of a dwelling.

Health:

Area of the bagua that represents the center and directly corresponds to you, the individual, as part of a community. In traditional Chinese feng shui as well as in Western feng shui, this area is located in the center of the room.

House blessing:

Ceremonial event meant to bring about heavenly blessings and protection for one's home.

I Ching:

The ancient Chinese book known as the "Book of Changes," on which much of feng shui theory is based.

Intention:

A broad and general wish that defines a value or desire.

Lao Tsu:

Chinese philosopher who is recognized as the author of the *Tao Te Ching*.

Legacy/Children:

Area of the bagua that represents your legacy, not only through your descendants who represent your physical creation, but also through expressions of your creativity and imagination. In traditional Chinese feng shui, this area is located west; in Western feng shui, it is the middle area of the right side of the room.

Luo pan:

Feng shui compass used in traditional Chinese feng shui schools.

Metal:

One of the five elements; it includes the following characteristics: Round, west, white, and metal shades. It represents morality, structure, and endings.

Missing space:

An area of the bagua that is missing in the layout of your home.

"Mouth of chi":

According to traditional feng shui, this is the entrance of your home.

North:

This direction is associated with the Water element. The influence of Water is that of deep thinking, communication, and transmission of ideas.

Poison arrow:

Sharp or pointed corners or objects. This angular design can make inhabitants feel on edge or even threatened.

Primary Imaging:

A newly developed process developed by Beverly Payeff. It can be used by Pyramid feng shui practitioners to identify shapes, forms, and colors that make a person feel safe and secure within a space.

Pyramid School:

Founded by Nancilee Wydra, this school addresses the Western culture. It incorporates basic feng shui tenets with the physical and social sciences.

Qi gong:

Movements that improve health and longevity as well as increase a sense of harmony; this term literally means "energy cultivation." It is one of the top healing modalities of traditional Chinese medicine.

Red Phoenix:

One of the four protective animals; it is associated with the south and the Fire element. It is located in front of a dwelling.

Reduction Cycle:

Cycle in which the elements, in a counterclockwise motion, reduce the preceding element and take from the original element. Fire reduces Wood; Wood reduces Water; Water reduces Metal; Metal reduces Earth; and Earth reduces Fire.

Relationships/Marriage:

Area of the bagua that represents all meaningful relationships, with the exception of your children. The influence of this station relates to being open, flexible, receptive, and making room for others. In traditional Chinese feng shui, this area is located southwest; in Western feng shui, it is the right upper corner of the room.

Sacred Geometry:

Belief that geometric shapes found in nature should be duplicated in architecture; this belief was used throughout the ancient world.

Self/Career:

Area of the bagua that represents self-expression and the path you venture on to reach self-actualization, which includes your profession or life mission. In traditional Chinese feng shui, this area is north; in Western feng shui, it is located at the bottom center of the room.

Sight:

One of the five senses, humans rely heaviest on the sense of sight to interpret their surroundings.

Smell:

One of the five senses, and the only sense that evokes a purely emotional response. Aromas are critical to the activities performed in a space and the level or quality of performance.

Sound:

One of the five senses, it is important to incorporate the sounds of nature into one's space and to eliminate loud and irritating noises.

South:

This direction is associated with the Fire element and it represents intelligence, spirit, human and animal life, passion, wisdom, charisma, and motivation.

Space clearing:

A ceremonial event used to bring about health, happiness, and prosperity within a space.

T'ai Chi Symbol:

A circle that looks like two interlocking swirls. One is black with a white dot, and the other is white with a black dot. It is often used to portray yin/yang.

Taoism:

An Eastern philosophy that professes humans achieve harmony and balance by living according to the laws of nature.

Taste:

One of the five senses, it is the most intimate of all the senses because you have to experience it up close.

Touch:

One of the five senses that can be experienced via physical contact or sensorial experience.

Symbols:

Any item that takes on profound meaning to the person who uses it. Symbols work on a deep, psychological level.

Water:

One of the five elements; it includes the following characteristics: Wavy, north, blue, and black. It yields to and conquers all.

West:

This direction is associated with the Metal element and it represents letting go, morality, ethics, precise thinking, structure, planning, and organization.

White Tiger:

One of the four protective animals, it represents the west and the Metal element. It is located on the right side of a dwelling.

Wisdom/Knowledge:

Area of the bagua that represents inner strength and growth of self. In traditional Chinese feng shui, this area is northeast; in Western feng shui, it is located in the bottom left corner.

Wood:

One of the five elements; it includes the following characteristics: Rectangle, east, and green tones. It represents growth, adventure, risk, and hope.

Yang:

Identified as active, light, and large, it is the complementary opposite of yin.

Yin:

Identified as passive, dark, and small, it is the complementary opposite of yang.

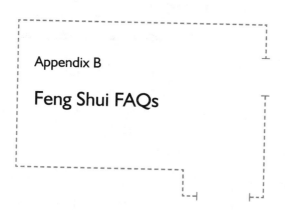

Appendix B

Feng Shui FAQs

Q What is feng shui?

A The Chinese proverb "as it is above, so it will be below" implies our interconnectedness with the natural world we inhabit. It is important to realize that our place in this system is central to our self-actualization. Feng shui explains how everything in our physical space can affect how we act, react, and interact. Feng shui believes that by shaping our environment, we will shape our lives. Often called the art of placement, feng shui explains how humans are influenced by their physical environment.

The words "feng shui" mean "wind and water." While the name feng shui is Chinese, the use of the physical environment to enhance life's successes is endemic to all cultures throughout history. Ancient people studied how wind and water behaved, so as to benefit from the ways of nature and avoid dangerous and destructive weather and geological forces. Although modern people are not as concerned with the weather as were our ancient counterparts, in many ways feng shui still acts as a tool for our personal and collective survival and growth.

Feng shui is an extraordinarily useful tool to help a person achieve what they want. It is based on a fundamental relationship, that of a person reacting to and interacting with their environment. Unfortunately, this is a relationship that is often overlooked. Considering that there are only two things consistently with us from birth until death, ourselves and some form of a physical environment around us, utilizing how we react to a physical environment makes sense. Altering a physical environment can keep us from repeating useless or detrimental patterns and taking advantage of what is always around us to assist us in reaching desired goals.

Q What are the roots of feng shui?

A Feng shui started some 200,000 years ago, at the juncture in history when humans ceased to be only hunters and gatherers. Hunters and gatherers did not alter nature; they were simply dependent on its bounty. Agriculture required humans to learn how sunlight, soil types, topography, wind, weather, and water impacted the crops. This understanding gave way to alteration and appropriate actions in order to thrive. At that point in history, when human beings became agrarian, they needed to learn how the environment affected their ability to survive. This was the first cognition of the impact of place, or feng shui.

Interestingly, hunter/gatherer groups typically numbered between 20 and 50 members, which sociologists today find is the same number of friendships and close acquaintances that most people have. Consider the people in your life with whom you feel close and you will discover that the number falls between 20 and 50. People then and now who do not have access to groups of about this size feel lonely on the inside and overwhelmed on the outside.

Fast forward to 6,000 years before the common era (B.C.E.) and evidence shows that the human race, as it evolved even more, adapted this discipline to site dwellings, palaces, government buildings, monuments, and even tombs auspiciously. A form of feng shui is practiced in all cultures. It is the Chinese, however, who have made it an integral part of their everyday life.

Communist politics in the Chinese culture caused the practice to go underground when Mao Tse-Tung banned it. Although not allowed in mainland China, feng shui continued to flourish in other Asian cities such as Hong Kong, where there was—and still is today—heavy use within the business community. Today, feng shui has made its way to the Western world. With new scientific discoveries, technology, and modern culture, it has evolved to an even more important influence on how we live our lives.

Q How did feng shui arrive in America?

A After World War II, China turned toward communism. Feng shui, along with Buddhism and Taoism, was judged obsolete and without value. The Cultural Revolution that followed banned religion altogether, a ban lifted in 1979. Nevertheless, the sophisticated body of feng shui knowledge was disrupted. As in the game of telephone, where something is repeated from one person to the next, the perfectly sensible teachings of feng shui became less and less sensible as it spread without benefit of continued growth and development. When the missionary Eitel wrote the first English language book on feng shui in 1873, it was a scathing report, calling feng shui a strange and unusual practice. This book was reprinted in 1974.

Migration to the West

Professor Lin Yun studied Tibetan Buddhist feng shui and related disciplines since his childhood. After moving to the USA, he established a feng shui school he called "Black Hat Sect," based on his traditional rules but more adapted to the West. His meeting with a Chinese language student, Sarah Rossbach, was fortuitous because she became interested in feng shui and wrote the first feng shui book published in America. Lin Yun and Sarah Rossbach carried the seeds that are evident in the popularity of feng shui today. Because of Lin Yun's early classes, many of the contemporary authors on feng shui have studied with him and written books from this Black Hat Sect perspective rather than the older, more scientifically sophisticated Chinese feng shui.

Pyramid Feng Shui

In the 1980s, Nancilee Wydra began to systematically trace other feng shui teachings backward in order to uncover the essence of this ancient practice. Her goal was to align the basic underpinnings with contemporary knowledge to give more veracity to feng shui. The underlying principles, which were rooted in nature and biology, were easily funneled into scientific research. After refining these ideas, she founded the Feng Shui Institute of America and published her first book, *Designing Your Happiness: A Contemporary Look at Feng Shui*. Currently, Nancilee has eight books written on feng shui and her ninth is in progress. The new model and practical approach that emerged focuses more on the way human beings filter information than on specific remedies used in prescribed ways.

Q What is unique about Pyramid school feng shui?

A The Pyramid model assumes that, although some ideas apply to all (or almost all) people in our great global world population, we learn much more from our own cultures. Every culture and time period is unique. Each time, place, and generation has its own talismans, memories of place, political history, and cultural icons. Today's world is not stable enough to permit generalizations from one generation to another. In addition, every individual within a culture has his or her own personal history, primal space images, color and smell associations, and life experiences. Thus, feng shui according to Wydra is a way of ascertaining the specific human filters that affect each person or entity and using place as a self-help tool to augment a person's life.

As we look at any aspect of human behavior, if we mistake something that is learned and culture-specific for a universal experience, we risk missing the real underlying principle involved. So translating feng shui principles from one culture and time to another, or even from one person to another, can severely limit the depth of a feng shui practice.

Pyramid feng shui, therefore, removes the traditional talismans to reveal the underlying principles, and applies these principles individually within a context of a culture. How do we see? How do we perceive others? What distances between people signify what meanings? What is the nature of our daily lives? How is space used? At what pace do we move in different circumstances? How do we react to colors?

In Pyramid feng shui, teachings of earlier traditions are used, but are scrutinized for their underlying or root veracity, before being accepted. For example, today, using nature's shapes may not exactly relate to buildings and roadways. Instead, we must learn to experience shapes, as those who live there would interpret them. Are they positive in terms of the people who reside there and what they are trying to accomplish? Shapes, sizes, and context are, after all, the silhouettes that frame ideas, meaning, and truths. For example, a city dweller's view of a colorful, large advertising sign can be either positive or negative depending upon the circumstances. If the person has difficulty kick-starting each day, he or she might find such a sign energizing. A person who has too many responsibilities and is always rushing around, however, might be pushed over an emotional and physical edge by the sign's additional stimulus and size.

The advice of the compass school is more challenging to apply in Western countries. Construction techniques that use extensive metal, the ubiquitous presence of electrical wiring, or even filling in teeth may interfere with accurate compass readings. Moreover, we usually do not have control over the orientation of our homes because of building codes, roads, and nearby structures. We cannot rotate a front door throughout the years to match the classic lo-pan readings. We cannot position a home anywhere on a lot because of setback requirements. We cannot easily move a kitchen to another location in our home. Even fences, which are recommended as beneficial in ancient feng shui, are often subject to detailed, but dissimilar regulation in each community.

However, we can and should use orientation as it relates to people's lifestyles and habits. Do they leave early before the sun rises? Do they return home when the setting sun is glaring over their rooftop as they walk the path to their front door? It is still auspicious to be synchronized with nature's cycle.

Q How do you become a feng shui professional?

A There are many professional certification programs throughout the country; however, we would caution anyone interested in pursuing a training program to pay close attention to the curriculum, the qualification of the teacher(s), and the course work. In particular, pay attention to whether or not a master status practitioner has developed the course of study and is instrumental in teaching. Most quality feng shui certification programs have a very demanding agenda involving independent study, research, and practical application.

The program where we received our training and certification was through the Feng Shui Institute of America (✍*www.wind water.com or 772-388-2085*). It promotes and teaches according to the Pyramid School of Feng Shui. The Pyramid School of Feng Shui incorporates the basic tenets of Chinese feng shui while incorporating modern and social physical science. In light of our contemporary expanded knowledge base, it makes sense that feng shui expands to include contemporary discoveries. Therefore, Pyramid feng shui, a contemporary explanation of the ancient forms, utilizes all social and physical sciences to support the ancient ideas while adding new discoveries in fields of all pertinent knowledge.

The Feng Shui Institute of America along with its professional arm, the Feng Shui Institute International (✍*www.fengshuiinstitute international.com or 614-837-8370*) offer the premium course of study and continuing education for feng shui professionals embracing cutting edge research in many fields applicable to feng shui.

Feng shui is a renaissance career because its field of practice encompasses all forms of knowledge. In preparing for professional status, you must study biology, cultural anthropology, psychology, and quantum psychics with an eye to understanding human behaviors and responses.

Unlike more traditional schools of feng shui, Pyramid feng shui developed in a climate of cultural diversity and unparalleled scientific advancements. Therefore, Pyramid feng shui embraces ideas and concepts unknown to the ancient Chinese. An example is primary memory of place, developed by Beverly Payeff, whose premise is that prior to a human's neo-cortex capability of storing memory through language (usually the first year of life), each of us forms impressions (positive and negative) that we have no access to later in life. These impressions constitute the shapes, placement, and colors that we prefer. Understanding how to access primary images of place gives architects, interior designers, realtors, and psychotherapists knowledge heretofore hidden from them.

If you are considering becoming a feng shui professional, we encourage you to specialize and include your existing areas of expertise. As in most professions, generalists are appreciated, but not prevalent.

Q How can feng shui be used by other professions?

A Feng shui can be applied to any profession. Some examples:

1. A career counselor can apply feng shui concepts when guiding clients by tying in career goals with intentions, and helping the client connect with a meaningful symbol that will support the client's career desires.
2. A psychologist might be more successful in helping a client if he or she had firsthand knowledge about the client's physical environment. A basic knowledge of physical barriers such as clutter, negative symbols, or inappropriate colors within the living space that hinder a client's emotional healing would be excellent information for any mental health professional.
3. A teacher could be experiencing problems with keeping children focused during reading sessions. A little feng shui can go a long way in a classroom by just repositioning desks and chairs.

4. Health professionals could use feng shui principles to foster a healing environment. For example, a cancer wing in a medical center could promote cheerfulness and healing by simply painting the walls a soft buttercream yellow. Nurses and doctors in hospitals would be able to comfort their patients by positioning them where they could connect with the outdoors.
5. A financial planner, having firsthand knowledge of feng shui, may be able to identify negative patterns in a person's life management by assessing their physical environment, and surmise how a client may handle their finances.
6. Architects, interior designers, and space planners would benefit from feng shui principles in order to better address the emotional and physical needs of their clients.

Q How do I find a qualified feng shui consultant?

A First, let's define "qualified consultant." If you are serious about using feng shui in your life, then you want to work with a consultant who has been through a rigorous certification program and has conducted more than one or two consultations. A qualified consultant will always list his or her method of training, including level of education. A consultant most likely would have studied under a mentor or even a feng shui master and should share that with you. Feng shui can be very powerful, and there are many underlying elements that someone reading a book or two would not be aware of. As a result, a recommendation that affects you negatively could be made.

When seeking out a qualified feng shui consultant in your area, use the Internet and search for feng shui organizations. They are located all over the world. The Feng Shui Institute International,

Inc. is favored by many, and its Web site is: *www.fengshuiinstitute international.com*. They have a membership roster of practitioners who have graduated from the Feng Shui Institute of America and are professional members—meaning they practice regularly and you can be assured you will get a professional trained in the field. You can also e-mail *fengshui@insight.rr.com* and you will be directed to a professional in your area.

You also can find names of practitioners in the bibliographies of books written by well-known masters in the field. Check your local library for these resources.

Q What is involved in a feng shui consultation?

A Feng shui consultations are different for each person or business. In general, however, an assessment is conducted first to determine the goals of the client. This is done through an in-depth interview, typically taking from one to two hours. The client should be prepared to discuss the goals or desires they wish to focus on. The more time given to this process, the more targeted the report can be. Photographs, notes, or sketches may be taken of your space. Landscape, furniture arrangement, artwork, and other artifacts are considered when preparing recommendations. Some practitioners will prepare a written report, which will include suggestions that will guide you in realizing your goals. Others will make immediate on-site recommendations.

Q I am an interior designer who is interested in feng shui; however, I do not want to become a professional feng shui consultant. Are there feng shui courses for professionals such as myself?

A The Feng Shui Institute of America offers numerous CEU courses for the design, medical, and other professional fields. FSIA has several CEU courses approved by the American Society of Interior Designers (ASID) and other design trade organizations. They can also develop CEU courses at the request of any professional trade association. Contact them at ✍*www.windwater.com* or 772-388-2085 to get a list of courses offered.

Q Are there educational classes given by a feng shui institute for the general public?

A Not only are classes available through various institutes around the world, but many feng shui professionals offer their own courses in their hometowns. Check the telephone books, local newspapers, and other various publications for a listing of individuals who offer feng shui consultations. You can also check with your local recreation centers, libraries, and community colleges for feng shui courses, or refer to the Feng Shui Institute International, Inc. Web site for a list of practitioners in your area (✍*www.fengshui instituteinternational.com*).

Q Is there a professional organization for feng shui professionals?

A In the United States, we recommend that you seek out membership in the Feng Shui Institute International, Inc. There are different levels of membership depending on the professional training of the consultant, similar to the levels established by ASID.

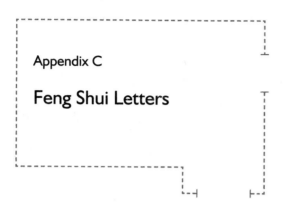

Appendix C

Feng Shui Letters

We write a regular column called "Feng Shui Today" for The Wellpoint (www.thewellpoint.com or 614-220-9355), a magazine devoted to a holistic approach to health, answering readers' letters. We have included here several of the most commonly posed questions.

De-Cluttering Your Life

Dear Connie and Sylvia,

Lately I have been feeling anxious and overwhelmed. I am experiencing problems on my job and feel like I need change in my life. The problem is that I can't seem to focus, making it difficult to consider a new direction for myself. What can you suggest to help me through this?

Please help.

Marianne J., Delaware, OH

Dear Marianne,

The Tao Te Ching, one of China's greatest philosophical classics, suggests that one devote time for regular reflection; only in this way can you quiet your mind to hear the lessons you are to learn.

It is difficult to quiet your mind if your environment is preventing you from enjoying that much needed downtime. The famous English novelist William Thackeray once said that the world is a looking glass; it reflects back to us what we hold in our own minds. Without looking at your physical living space, we'll venture to guess that a lot of clutter and disorganization exists in your home and therefore, is reflecting disorganization in your thoughts and emotions.

You need to get focused so you can do some deep reflection to search for a new direction in your life. Let's start with getting rid of objects that no longer serve a purpose or inspire you. Clear all unnecessary clutter from your home. Containerize, label, sort, and file your paperwork so that your paper mess does not continuously busy your mind.

Simplify! Simplify! Simplify! Once this is done, your home should begin to feel a lot lighter, airier, and less overwhelming.

The physical change in your environment will also reflect in your emotional state of mind.

Now we can make suggestions to help you be more reflective:

1. Bring the Water element into your space. This can be accomplished in many ways. If you have a window that overlooks a yard, add a bird bath, some purple or lilac flowers to attract butterflies, and soft greenery. Place a chair by this window and sit in it daily to connect with nature and your thoughts. Have a journal beside you to write down those thoughts for future reference.

2. Place a small water fountain that reverberates soft sounds of water trickling or flowing. The sound of water flowing causes us to relax and reflect on less stressful things in life. It renews us and regenerates our creativity.

3. Soften straight lines in your environment such as corner edges of tables and walls by adding tall plants against walls and vines over table or bookshelf edges; you can also hang soft sheer fabric over these edges.

4. Surround yourself with books and writings of others who have reflected upon their own lives and written about it.

5. Bring the Metal element into your environment to promote focus. Any small metal object such as a brass planter or a metal-framed picture will work.

6. Follow the path of the moon for a month. This will take you outside at night where it is more quiet and dark; both of these qualities will help still your mind. It will also remind you of the many cycles of nature and help you realize that life is about change. Be like nature and go with the flow; resistance to change is never the answer.

Nature's Lessons for a Career Change

Dear Connie and Sylvia,

I am going to start a new career as a massage therapist. This is a big change as I used to be an elementary school teacher. I have read that feng shui can help a person with career changes. What tips can you give me?

Thanking you in advance,
Barbara H., Cleveland, OH

Dear Barbara,

Feng shui can definitely help! First of all, life is about change and transitions. As this occurs, you grow and gain wisdom. Even though you might be anxious to leave the teaching field, it is important to reflect on the benefits you received and the contributions you made. Your role as a teacher is invaluable to all future endeavors, and you take skills that can be transferred to your new career.

One of the main themes of feng shui is that of change. Feng shui is a philosophy based on the laws of nature, and the best way to understand change is to study nature. Just as nature moves in cycles, so must we, or else we become stagnant. Moving from one career to another is like moving from one chapter of your life to the next.

So that your new venture goes smoothly, we suggest you take your lessons from the Five Element Cycle, which is also referred to as the Human Life Cycle. The five elements are found in the natural world and define all existence. They are Wood, Fire, Earth, Metal, and Water. Each of the elements has a corresponding color, time of day, season, shape, etc. More important, each element exerts an energy and influence. For this time of transition, you need to tap into Earth energy.

The influence of Earth is that of stability, a strong sense of foundation, and equilibrium. Indian summer is the season of Earth and is seen as a time of transition between two seasons. Earth is also associated with mid-afternoon, another time in between. Just as Earth finds itself "in between," so do you, as you are in between two careers. Move slowly, step cautiously, rest, and nurture yourself. By doing this, you will not only start anew, you will emerge a new person—one with direction and passion. Keep in mind that transition is different from change. Transition demands that you first become still, rest, and seek out the quiet center of your soul. Face west and meditate. This is the direction that will inspire you to let go so that you can move on. Adjust your physical environment by surrounding yourself with Earth features. The colors of Earth are yellow, brown, beige, terra cotta, peach, and other similar hues. Items that represent Earth include rocks, ceramics, crystals, and sand. Earth landscapes, photos of the Southwest, and stone sculptures are good art choices.

Since you will be crossing from one career to another, prepare yourself to cross a new threshold. Thresholds are like bridges we cross over into another realm of our lives. They underline the transition from one place to another, much like a rite of passage. Each rite of passage represents crossing a threshold to another chapter in a person's life. It's a ritualistic way to mark life's critical moments in time.

Have your thresholds clearly identified in your home. Metaphorically, your life will reflect what you physically surround yourself with. If your thresholds are obstructed and cluttered in any way, so will each threshold in your life be obstructed and cluttered.

The Dining Room Dilemma

Dear Sylvia and Connie,

I have attended some of your workshops and have found them very helpful in creating a home that meets my needs. I am running into one problem with a particular room—my dining room. The room is too small for a large group of people and I use my large kitchen for big dinners. This means that the dining room usually sits unused except to collect paperwork, bills, and books that I am hoping to read. Since I have no designated area where I can do paperwork, the dining room is becoming my dumping ground. I need help. Any feng shui suggestions to help my ailing dining room?

Sincerely,

Melissa S., Columbus, OH

Dear Melissa,

Two things are apparent: First, your dining room is not serving your needs and second, your bills and books are screaming for your attention.

An important thing to remember with feng shui is that every room must be used. A room that just sits there is like a stagnant energy—with little movement or circulation, your dining room is fast becoming an unhealthy space. To compound things, you are creating a clutter trap, which eventually affects your emotional, spiritual, and physical well-being. Physical clutter leads to mind clutter.

Here are a few suggestions:

1. Turn your unused dining room into an office/library. When choosing your office furniture, choose items with rounded corners and with drawers that can serve as filing

cabinets. Ideally, you should position your desk so that your back is to a solid surface. Next, while sitting at your desk, you need to be able to see the entry door, preferably in the diagonal corner.

2. Tall bookcases should not be placed directly in front of you; you might feel overwhelmed or oppressed. Also, don't stuff the shelving and fill up all the space as it will create tension and make you feel "crowded."

3. Create a reading area with a comfortable chair, small side table, and lamp. Use a full-spectrum light bulb in the lamp. Full-spectrum lighting, although artificial, comes closest to duplicating the rays of the sun. In feng shui, one goal is to bring the outside into our living spaces; full-spectrum lighting is a good way to "bring in a little sunshine."

4. Bring in plants—they will help clean the air. Choose plants with rounded leaves or ones that sway easily in a gentle breeze. Lush, healthy foliage can serve as a metaphor for abundance.

Hope this helps and good luck with your new room.

Appendix D

A Feng Shui Plan

The following figures, and the bagua on page 52, should be useful as you formulate your Feng Shui Plan for your home or office. Use a pencil and graph paper to sketch out a basic floor plan for either your whole home or a specific room. Then, arrange the sample furnishings until you find the design that works best for you—before you start moving furniture!

Office

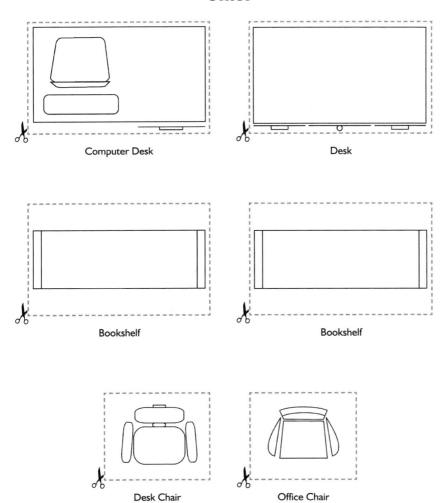

Computer Desk

Desk

Bookshelf

Bookshelf

Desk Chair

Office Chair

Bedroom

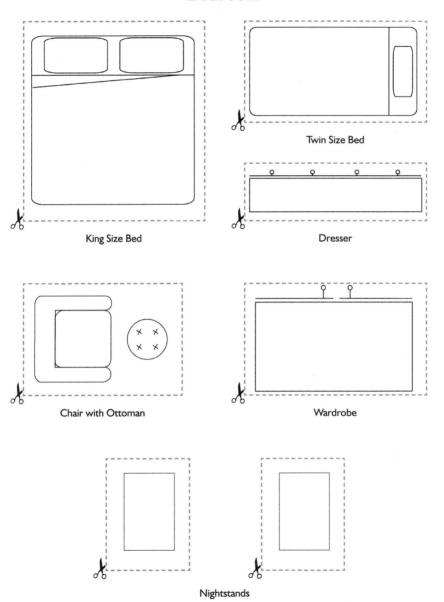

King Size Bed

Twin Size Bed

Dresser

Chair with Ottoman

Wardrobe

Nightstands

Dining Room

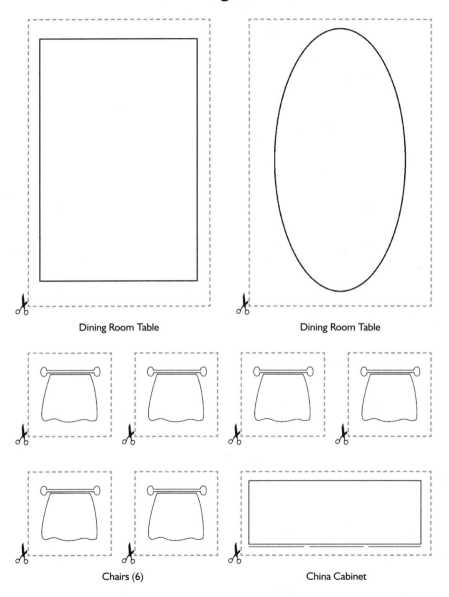

Dining Room Table

Dining Room Table

Chairs (6)

China Cabinet

Living Room

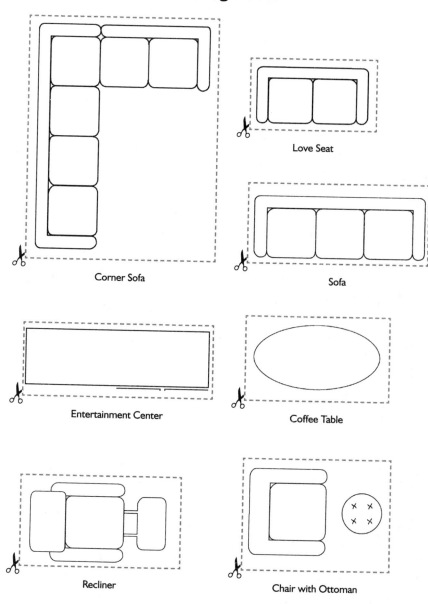

Corner Sofa

Love Seat

Sofa

Entertainment Center

Coffee Table

Recliner

Chair with Ottoman

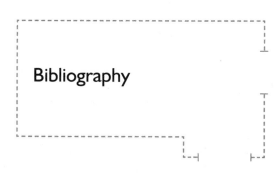

Bibliography

Please consider this a suggested reading list for those of you interested in learning more about feng shui and related fields.

Ackerman, Diane. *A Natural History of the Senses* (Vintage Books, 1990).

Aronson, Tara. *Simplify Your Household* (Readers Digest/Weldon Owen Publication, 1998).

Aslett, Don. *Lose 200 LBS. This Weekend* (Marsh Creek Press, 2000).

Baker, M.D., Sidney MacDonald. *The Circadian Prescription* (Penguin-Putnam, Inc., 2000).

Balter, Gaylah. *Clean Your Clutter, Clear Your Life* (The Learning Tree, 2001).

Bartlett, Sarah. *Feng Shui for Entertaining* (Vista-Orion Books, 1999).

Beinfield, Harriet, L.Ac., and Efrem Korngold, L.Ac., O.M.D. *Between Heaven and Earth: A Guide to Chinese Medicine* (Ballantine Books, 1991).

Bennett-Goleman, Tara. *Emotional Alchemy: How the Mind Can Heal the Heart* (Harmony Books, 2001).

Brown, Simon. *Practical Feng Shui at Work* (Barnes & Noble Books, 1998)

Campbell, Don. *The Mozart Effect* (Avon Books, 1997).

Campbell, Joseph. *The Power of Myth* (Anchor Books, 1988).

Chiazzari, Suzy. *The Healing Home* (Trafalgar Square Publishing, 1998).

Dunne, Catherine Bailly. *Interior Designing for all Five Senses* (Golden Books, 1998).

Hale, Gill. *The Practical Encyclopedia of Feng Shui* (Lorenz Books, 1999).

Hallowell, Edward M., M.D. *Connect* (Pantheon Books, 1999).

Hunt, Valerie, Dr. *Infinite Mind: Science of the Human Vibrations of Consciousness* (Malibu Publishing, 1996).

Jacobson, Max, Murray Silverstein, and Barbara Winslow. *Patterns of Home: The Ten Essentials of Enduring Design* (Taunton Press, 2002).

Kellert, Stephen R., and Edward O. Wilson, ed. *The Biophilia Hypothesis* (Island Press, 1993).

Kingston, Karen. *Clear Your Clutter with Feng Shui* (Broadway Books, 1998).

Lieberman OD, PhD, FCSO, et.al. *Light Years Ahead—An Illustrated Guide to Full Spectrum and Colored Light in Mind Body Healing,* (Brian Joeseph Breiling, 1996)

Linn, Denise. *Feng Shui for the Soul* (Hay House, Inc., 1999).

Magee, Vishu. *Archetype Design* (Random House, 1999).

Niven, David, Ph.D. *The 100 Simple Secrets of Happy People* (HarperCollins, 2000).

Passoff, Michelle. *Lighten Up! Free Yourself from Clutter* (HarperCollins, 1998).

Pert, Candace. *Molecules of Emotion—The Science Behind Mind-Body Medicine* (Touchstone, 1997).

Rossbach, Sarah. *Feng Shui, The Chinese Art of Placement* (Penguin, 1983).

Rossbach, Sarah. *Interior Design with Feng Shui* (Penguin, 1987).

Roszak, Theodore, Mary E. Gomes, and Allen D. Kanner, eds. *Ecopsychology* (Sierra Club Books, 1995).

Stocking, Jerry. *Thinking Clearly* (Moose Ear Press, 1997).

Swan, James A. *The Power of Place* (Theosophical Publishing House, 1991).

Thompson, Angel. *Feng Shui: How to Achieve the Most Harmonious Arrangement of Your Home and Office* (St. Martin's Press, 1996).

Too, Lillian. *The Complete Illustrated Guide to Feng Shui* (Barnes & Noble Books, 1996).

Venolia, Carol. *Healing Environments* (Celestial Arts, 1988).

Wong, Eva. *Feng Shui: The Ancient Wisdom of Harmonious Living for Modern Times* (Shambhala Publications, Inc. 1996).

Wydra, Nancilee. *Feng Shui: The Book of Cures* (Contemporary Books, 1996).

Wydra, Nancilee. *Feng Shui Goes to the Office* (Contemporary Books, 2000).

Wydra, Nancilee. *Feng Shui and How to Look Before You Love* (Contemporary Books, 1998).

INDEX